W9-BCT-878

Home Schooling

Home Schooling

Parents as Educators

Maralee Mayberry
J. Gary Knowles
Brian Ray
Stacey Marlow

CORWIN PRESS, INC.
A Sage Publications Company
Thousand Oaks, California 91320

For information, address:

 Corwin Press, Inc.
A Sage Publications Company
2455 Teller Road
Thousand Oaks, California 91320

SAGE Publications Ltd.
6 Bonhill Street
London EC2A 4PU
United Kingdom

SAGE Publications India Pvt. Ltd.
M-32 Market
Greater Kailash I
New Delhi 110 048 India

Printed in the United States of America

Library of Congress Cataloging-in-Publication Data

Home schooling: Parents as educators / Maralee Mayberry . . . [et al.].
   p. cm.
  Includes bibliographical references and index.
  ISBN 0-8039-6075-1 (acid-free paper).—ISBN 0-8039-6076-X (pbk.:
  acid-free paper)
  1. Home schooling—United States.   I. Mayberry, Maralee.

  LC40.H65 1995
  649'.68—dc20   94-23543

This book is printed on acid-free paper.

95 96 97 98 99 10 9 8 7 6 5 4 3 2 1

Corwin Press Production Editor: Tricia K. Bennett

Contents

Detailed Contents

List of Tables

Preface

There is no one who can love, nurture, and teach our kids better than we can. We know their individual talents and needs.

—28-year-old home school mother, Washington

The growing attractiveness of educating school-aged children at home cannot be denied. It is predicted that by the turn of the century approximately 2% of the school-aged population in the United States could be children taught at home (Ray, 1992b). Given this trend, it is likely that home schools are a permanent feature of our landscape.

We believe that the time is ripe for a detailed account of home schooling. This book covers the home education movement, the parents who teach their children at home, and the social and legal contexts that shape their relationship to local educational communities. We do not provide information on "how to" home school nor do we focus on the educational curricula parent educators use in their home instruction programs. Rather, our intention is to encourage different ways of thinking about home schools and the parents who operate them. Our goal is to present a vision of home education that reflects its multidimensional nature, *not* to advocate home schooling as the "best" educational approach.

We acknowledge that some home education parents view public schools as an unimaginable evil. We also acknowledge that some professional educators maintain an anti-home school stance. Similarly, home school parents and professional educators often disagree about how and where children learn best. However, these two groups also agree about many educational issues. In this book, our approach is to highlight these issues, thereby enhancing the possible development of cooperative relations between professional educators and home educators. We hope that this approach will be of interest to home school parents, school teachers and administrators, school board members, educational and social science researchers, and scholars.

Overview of the Book

In Chapter 1, we discuss what years of research has taught us about the parents who choose to educate their children at home. We also describe the study from which this book is drawn. Conducting research on home education, as we discovered, is often difficult and requires the researcher to invest time and effort to gain trust in the home school community. Chapter 2 begins our exploration of the home school phenomenon. Here we focus on the home education movement with respect to five phases, illustrating its complex and fluid nature: contention, confrontation, cooperation, consolidation, and compartmentalization. We show that despite the diverse and often discordant views of parent educators and their advocates, the movement remains remarkably unified.

In Chapters 3 through 5, we turn our attention to home education parents and their perspectives. Chapter 3 demonstrates that parent educators are not a monolithic group. Rather, they come from a wide range of educational and economic backgrounds and hold a variety of political and religious beliefs. In Chapter 4 we present the actual stories of several parent educators, illustrating the complex, yet rich meanings that they associate with the activity of home schooling. We examine the issue of cooperation between home schools and formal schools in Chapter 5. Many parent educators are interested in taking advantage of the various resources that cooperative programs offer. We show, however, that participation in these programs is contingent upon the degree to which parent educators believe that the autonomy of their home instruction programs might be restricted.

In Chapter 6 we provide a different perspective on home education. In this chapter, we turn our attention to school superintendents' interpretations of home school regulations and their views about parent educators. We demonstrate that neither the policies governing home instruction nor the various rationales parents have for teaching their children at home are clearly understood by many district superintendents. Effective policy implementation, we argue, is dependent on the ability of superintendents to make thoughtful, informed, and viable decisions.

In the final chapter, we briefly explore the intersections between social life, school life, and family life. In this chapter we also pose a number of issues and questions designed to stimulate the thinking of home education parents, professional educators, and educational policy makers. We believe that cooperative and reciprocal relations can be established if serious consideration is given to the issues and questions we raise in this chapter. We also suggest directions for future research.

Acknowledgments

The research represented in this volume began with a grant from the U.S. Department of Education, which we wish to thank for its support. Since that time, many people helped make this book possible. We want to thank the numerous school district administrators and members of home school organizations who provided us with valuable information and introduced us to many parent educators, the people about whom this book is written.

We want to acknowledge our colleagues at our respective universities who read parts of the manuscript, and provided encouragement and assistance. Among them, we thank Melissa Monson for her help with data analysis, Paul Davis and Barry Siegel for the hours that they spent completing the tedious task of transcribing interviews and organizing survey mailings and responses, James Muchmore and Kim Browning for their help in the early phases of this project, Christopher J. Klicka for providing up-to-date legal information about home education, and Veona Hunsinger and Susie Lafrentz for their administrative and secretarial help. Many organizers of home education networking groups helped us distribute surveys, and we are indebted to them.

We also thank Gracia Alkema and Ann McMartin of Corwin Press; Linda Montgomery, Principal of King's High School, Seattle; and an anonymous reviewer for helpful and insightful comments. Their suggestions assisted considerably in helping us think through various aspects of this book.

Maralee Mayberry would like to thank Peg Rees for her encouragement, support, and editorial help. Gary Knowles thanks Ardra Cole of the Ontario Institute for Studies in Education for her critique of his work. He also thanks Ardra and Carol Muller for their editorial assistance. Brian Ray thanks his wife, Betsy, for her Christian love and insightful reading and comments on the draft manuscript.

Finally, we wish to give special thanks to the many home education parents who have allowed us into their lives. Without their trust and support, research on home education would not exist. We dedicate this book to them.

About the Authors

Maralee Mayberry is Associate Professor of Sociology at the University of Nevada, Las Vegas. Her major interests lie in the areas of sociology of education, political sociology, and gender studies. Her most recent book is *Effective Educational Environments* (Corwin Press, 1992), written with Jean Stockard. Her articles pertaining to home schooling appear in *The School Community Journal, Home School Researcher, Continuing Higher Education Review, The Urban Review, Educational Review,* and *Education and Urban Society.*

J. Gary Knowles is Assistant Professor of Education at the University of Michigan, Ann Arbor. His research interests center on issues of teacher development in addition to home education. He has recently published articles in *Teachers College Record, American Journal of Education, International Journal of Qualitative Studies in Education, Curriculum Inquiry,* and *Teacher Education Quarterly.* In 1988, he edited a special issue of *Education and Urban Society* that explored home education research and issues. With R. V. Bullough and N. A. Crow, he wrote *Emerging as a Teacher,* and with A. L. Cole and C. Presswood, *Through Preservice Teachers' Eyes.*

Brian Ray is Associate Professor of Science and Education at Western Baptist College, President of the National Home Education Research Institute (NHERI), and founding editor of the refereed quarterly journal *Home School Researcher.* Many of his articles appear in home education magazines as well as in the *Journal of Research in Science Teaching* and *Education and Urban Society.* His current research focuses on home education and science education.

Stacey Marlow is Assistant Professor of Educational Administration at the University of Hawaii, Manoa. Her research interests include school administrators' implementation of educational policy (including home education policy) and alternative preparation programs for school administrators. She has published articles in the *American Journal of Education* and *Education and Urban Society.*

1
Learning About Home Schools

When you say "home school" to the people in this area, they think immediately that we're a group doing weird things, and I don't understand why.

—38-year-old home school father, Utah

I think children should have time to concentrate on what is meaningful to them and on what is going to help them develop into secure productive adults. Going to [public] school makes this difficult, not only because of the time and energy it requires, but also because of the continuous peer pressure to act or not act in a certain way, or to participate or not in certain types of activities. I consider that our children attend school in a sense—it's just that we choose our own subjects.

—45-year-old home school mother, Nevada

Home education has been our primary research domain for a number of years. We each spent many hours talking with, listening to, and learning from parents who teach their children at home. We also volunteered time consulting with home education organizations and working on committees established to develop home school policy recommendations.

In our work with parent educators, we became convinced that the activity of home schooling is woven into the very fabric of family life. For home school parents, playing a primary role in their children's education is fundamental to their sense of what it means to be a parent. We also were struck by the myriad of beliefs, values, and views that shaped the decision of parents to establish home schools. We met those who believed it was their "God-given right" to be responsible for their children's education. They established home instruction programs based upon their particular Christian religious and philosophical orientations. Conversely, we met parents who were committed to providing their children with an educational environment and curriculum that emphasized New Age or countercultural beliefs and lifestyles.

Diverse pedagogical concerns also played a role in shaping parents' decision to teach their children at home. Concerns about children's physical safety, academic and moral training, and socialization experiences led some parents to seriously consider the option of home education. Others began home schools for the explicit purpose of establishing high academic standards. They believed that their intimate familiarity with their children's learning styles and individual talents would allow them to develop educational programs superior to those available in formal schools.

In the course of our research, we also discovered that parents and professional educators often disagreed about how and where children learn best. Consequently, the relationships between these groups were often filled with tension and misunderstanding. We found that the professional community routinely distorted the goals, intentions, and abilities of home school parents. Likewise, parent educators often misread the concerns professional educators expressed and unnecessarily perceived their comments as a threat to the home school community.

Over the years, our professions have offered us the opportunity to be intricately involved in a wide range of discussions about home education. Not surprising, we have found that the topic of home schooling arouses strong feelings, both for and against. For instance, opponents of home education frequently voice a concern about the social development of children educated at home. They argue that interaction with other children is a vital part of formal schooling that cannot be addressed in the home. Home school parents, on the other hand, often claim that the current social environment of formal schools is actually a compelling argument for operating a home school. They argue that the home is a safer and more congenial learning environment. Furthermore, home schooling is challenged repeatedly on the grounds that many parents are not qualified to educate their own children and that any attempt to do so will only "damage" children academically. In response to this charge, parent educators quickly point to numerous studies that suggest home-educated children, when compared to children educated in public schools, score as well as or better on standardized achievement tests (see Ray, 1990b, for a review of this research).

These experiences led us to the challenge of providing a more complex account of home schools and the parents who operate them. The issues we address in this book include both parent educators' and school superintendents' understandings of home schooling, as well as the development of the home school movement. We also acknowledge the broad cultural and ideological variations in the home school population. Furthermore, we recognize the intersections between families, schools, and communities, delineating the challenge posed by the home school movement to systems of formal schooling. We believe that this approach will not only broaden the understanding of why increasing numbers of parents are choosing to teach their children at home but also help inform future policy decisions. In the following section, we discuss the study from which much of this book is drawn.

The Study: Home School Parents and School District Superintendents in Washington, Utah, and Nevada

We became familiar with the families and school district superintendents who inspired this book during a 2-year period, 1990 to 1991. At the outset, we met school officials charged with home school affairs and talked to many members of various home school organizations. Our meetings and conversations brought us closer to many home education parents and school district superintendents.

Our efforts were rewarded. We were provided with the mailing, membership, and registration lists that allowed us to study a wide range of parent educators from Washington, Utah, and Nevada. Moreover, our frequent discussions with school superintendents in each state helped to legitimate our project, increasing the likelihood that other school district officials would participate in the project. Despite our efforts, however, and for reasons discussed below, the nature of home education makes obtaining a representative sample problematic. Indeed, to date, no sample of parent educators can be regarded confidently as representative of the total population (see Lines, 1991b, for a detailed discussion of this issue).

Research Dilemmas

For both ideological and legal reasons, many parent educators do not wish to participate in studies about home schools. Some parents, for instance, believe that home education researchers are associated with governmental agencies and fear that researchers' findings may be used to prevent the future operation of home schools (Divoky, 1983; Lines, 1982). Other parents may be operating home schools "underground" (i.e., without being properly registered with a local school district) or in states that strictly enforce compulsory education codes (Harris & Fields, 1982; Lines, 1985b). Not only are these parents extremely difficult to locate, but due to the unauthorized status of their home school, they are highly unlikely to respond to social research surveys. Thus research on home education families is limited primarily to those parents who registered their home school and developed a sense of trust about the researchers conducting the study.

Another issue associated with research on home education is raised by clusters of parent educators who oppose the intrusion into their lives by researchers—particularly those conducting survey research (Kaseman & Kaseman, 1990, 1991). One of the indictments often raised by these parents against survey research is its potential inability to represent the complexities of home education. In addition, some parents are very hesitant about research activities that may not adequately portray the intensive process of home education.

Consequently, those involved in home education must largely identify themselves to the researchers. Just criticism has been directed at some home school research reports because of the lack of control researchers have over the selection of home education participants. We employed strategies to help ameliorate this situation and the problems discussed above. We addressed the problem of research resistance by making personal appeals to the leadership and constituents of networking groups for the purpose of encouraging their participation. We also made ourselves available to the home school communities in each state by providing workshops and other forms of presentation and consultation. Thus each of us acted in some way as either consultants or advisers to home school organizations. We believed that our involvement in home education communities would remove the objections that some parent educators had about participating in the project. In addition, we attempted to help potential respondents feel at ease with the process of data collection, making available a cost-free telephone contact (i.e., collect calling) for the purposes of their inquiry.

So What Did We Achieve?

The first phase of our study was designed to obtain demographic and attitudinal information about parents and their home schools. We combined the registration lists provided by school districts, home school organizations, and networking groups in each state and mailed a 56-item (290 variables) questionnaire to 6,064 families. We received a response from 1,497. Although a 25% response rate seemed low, after analyzing our data we found that our sample included parent educators with a range of motivations for operating home schools, including those motivations identified in previous research (see Mayberry, 1988; Pitman, 1987; Van Galen, 1986; Wartes, 1988). We also found that the demographic, religious, and political characteristics of the parents responding to our survey displayed some degree of variation. These findings increased our confidence that the convenience sample included a wide range of home education families. We attribute this diversity to having obtained registration and membership lists from school districts and home school organizations that service parent educators from various ideological and demographic backgrounds. Nonetheless, our conclusions are based primarily upon the responses of parents who are part of the organized and legally authorized home school movement.

The second phase of our study was designed to give us deeper insight into the past and present experiences that led parents to the decision of teaching their children at home. Our years of involvement in social and educational research made it apparent that the story of any group is best told by its members. Thus we conducted semistructured, in-depth interviews with home education families in three states.

We selected 36 families (12 families in each state) to interview. Those parents who were interviewed were chosen through the process of "dimensional sampling" (see Arnold, 1970, for a detailed discussion of this sampling technique). The criterion used to select parent educators was the ability of the family to represent various combinations of significant analytical dimensions. For instance, one family might represent the religiously motivated, highly educated, and politically conservative dimension of the home school population; another family, the pedagogically motivated, less educated, and politically liberal dimension. The combination of families that we interviewed represents the diversity of parent educators who responded to our survey. If a family did not agree to be interviewed, another family representing that particular dimension was selected. We found that the interview transcriptions complemented the written comments that parent educators made on the survey; together, they provided a vast number of narrative responses that are integrated, verbatim, throughout this book.

The third phase of our study was designed to elicit information from school district superintendents. We designed a mail survey with the explicit purpose of obtaining information about the laws and policies governing home schools in each district. The first sections of the survey provided information about the characteristics of the school district, the facilities that were made available to home school students and their parents, and the laws and policies that governed home schools in the particular school districts. The survey also examined how superintendents both interpreted and implemented governance requirements. In addition, it explored superintendents' perceptions of home-educated students and their parents.

The superintendents were asked to furnish relevant documents pertaining to policy statements, court decisions, and special administrative rules or regulations. The survey questionnaire was mailed to all 307 superintendents employed in Washington, Utah, and Nevada, and the 118 superintendents who returned our survey constituted a 38% response rate. The representativeness of the sample is questionable. It is difficult to know why the other superintendents did not return the questionnaire, or if their responses would have significantly altered our findings. The superintendents who did return the survey, however, were fairly well distributed geographically throughout each state.[1]

Our findings are, therefore, based on a convenience, nonrepresentative sample. Fully aware of the problems associated with convenience samples, we took much care throughout this book to represent the diverse viewpoints of the parent educators and school officials who participated in the study. We believe that the wide range of information we collected can help us begin to identify areas of agreement between parent educators and school administrators— an implicit theme of this book.

Why Is Understanding Home Education Important?

Lines (1991b) estimated that by the early 1980s, 60,000 to 125,000 children were receiving home-based instruction. During the 1990 to 1991 school year, she estimated that the number of children taught at home grew to 250,000 to 360,000 (Lines, 1991a). More recently, Ray (1992a) estimated that in 1992 approximately 375,000 school-aged children were home educated, and during the 1993 to 1994 academic year between 450,000 and 800,000 children were educated at home. Moreover, Ray's (1992a) analysis of statewide data demonstrated that in recent years the number of home schools nationwide grew about 15% per year.[2]

This tremendous growth challenges us to take seriously the topic of home education. A promising body of literature emerged in recent years responding to this challenge. Social scientists from a variety of disciplines documented the increased popularity of home education (e.g., Allis, 1990; Gordon & Gordon, 1990) and addressed various aspects of home education, including legal issues (Harris & Fields, 1982; Klicka, 1990; Lines, 1983; Mayberry & Gerdes, 1989; Richardson & Zirkel, 1991; Yastrow, 1990); historical and sociological concerns (Bates, 1991; Knowles, Marlow, & Muchmore, 1992; Mayberry, 1988, 1989; Mayberry & Knowles, 1989; Shepherd, 1986); learning processes (Mayberry, 1993; Quine & Marek, 1988; Treat, 1990); policy implications (Knowles, 1989; Knowles, Mayberry, & Ray, 1991; Lines, 1986); student achievement (Ray, 1988, 1990a, 1990b; Wartes, 1990a, 1990b); and home-educated students' social and emotional adjustment (Delahooke, 1986; Hedin, 1991; Montgomery, 1989; Taylor, 1987).

These studies, however, were limited by their small sample sizes, sometimes inappropriate sampling procedures, and an inability to compare the characteristics of home school parents with larger state or national populations (see Lines, 1991b). Furthermore, previous studies focused almost exclusively on single issues and failed to address the multifaceted nature of home education. This book begins to fill that gap. In the next chapter, we begin our journey into the world of home education by exploring the fluid and complex nature of the home school movement.

Notes

1. For a more detailed description of the methodology employed in this study, see Knowles, Mayberry, and Ray (1991).

2. Some observers of the home education movement estimated the number of children being home schooled in the United States during the 1980s to be in excess of one million (Moore, 1983; Naisbitt, 1982). Lines (1991b) argued, however, that these early estimates were based on faulty assessment procedures. Her estimates used the enrollment numbers of home school curricular package distributors and adjustments for those children not enrolled. The estimations of Ray (1992a) relied heavily on Lines's (1991a, 1991b) techniques.

2

The Home Education Movement

WHAT WE KNOW

Home schooling is a fast-growing movement in American education that shows no sign of slackening.

—Toch et al. (1991, p. 73)

During the 1980s, the growth of home education was considerable in both its momentum and visibility. There is no question that home education is a social movement (Sexson, 1988). In this chapter, we discuss the evolving milieu of the contemporary home school movement. Particular attention is paid to several features of the movement that characterize its growth and development. For instance, the movement developed rapidly during a period when criticisms of public education were numerous and well publicized. As home schools became more numerous, legal confrontations and judicial activity increased, but at the same time home education took its first steps toward gaining acceptance and legitimacy. The movement's

AUTHORS' NOTE: Portions of this chapter were previously published in J. G. Knowles, S. Marlow, and J. Muchmore, "Trom Pedagogy to Ideology: Origins and Phases of Home Education in the United States, 1970-1990," *American Journal of Education, 100* (February 1992): 195-235. © 1992 by The University of Chicago. All rights reserved.

continued growth was fueled by the extensive and complex organizational networks that were established locally, nationally, and internationally. Currently, the movement's organizational structure is becoming increasingly factionalized, yet its unity and strength is still evidenced by successful lobbying and legal efforts on behalf of home school parents. These features suggest that the contemporary home school movement is not simply a return to educational practices of the past, but a genuine and justifiable alternative in today's proreform educational climate.[1]

A Movement in Motion

The 1990s have witnessed the public's growing acceptance of home schools and the parents who operate them. Prior times, however, have not always been easy. During the past 20 years, the public and media have often viewed home schooling as a subversive educational activity carried out by fanatics or idealists, often surreptitiously or underground. Some parent educators have even been jailed or fined for teaching their children at home. For example, the following incident took place in the state of Iowa: "A fundamentalist minister walked into jail Saturday to serve 30 days for educating his daughter without state approval" ("Pastor Jailed for Home Educating," 1987, p. A5). More dramatically, the case of Utahan John Singer emerged as an example of the lengths to which opposing sides would go to prove their point about whether or not parents had the right to operate a home school. Singer was killed in a "gun battle" in 1979 after police arrested him on charges related to his Mormon/polygamist religion and the home education of his children (Fleisher & Freedman, 1983; Williamson, 1979).

In more recent years, home education has taken on a new image, one that is now approaching legitimacy. The most significant factor behind the growing public acceptance of home schools is the establishment of a vast array of support systems and networking organizations. Over the years, the work of parent educators has gained credibility and has reached an ever-widening audience. One home school parent in Washington state illustrated this point:

Last week at the beauty shop the woman, who has been cutting my hair for several years, remarked, "When you first told me that you taught your kids at home, I'd never heard of anyone doing that, and thought it was really strange. But, I'll bet there are four or five people who come into the shop now who teach their own kids. They belong to groups with other families who are teaching their kids at home, and they tell us about it—it's really pretty interesting, and it doesn't seem as strange any more."

This example reflects the public's changing sentiment toward home education. Perceptions of home schools have changed dramatically over the years; however, vestiges of previous attitudes still remain. In the remainder of this chapter, we examine the evolution of the home education movement, paying particular attention to the impact that public attitudes have on its development. The movement is best described by five overlapping phases: contention, confrontation, cooperation, consolidation, and compartmentalization.

Contention

During the late 1960s and early 1970s, the work of educational critics such as John Holt (1969) and Ivan Illich (1970) fueled an air of dissatisfaction with public education. Other vocal critics of public education included social scientists such as Marilyn Gittell, David Rogers, and Frank Riessman; writers and journalists like Charles Silberman, George Leonard, Nat Hentoff, and George Dennison; and practicing teachers such as Jonathan Kozol, Herbert Kohl, and James Herndon. The work produced by these critics was driven by what they perceived as the deplorable condition of public education. Consequently, during this period, the documentation and subsequent publicity about the failings of public schools was unprecedented.

The increasing contention over public schools was not, however, merely a unique response to a specific set of circumstances. Recognition must also be given to the long and cyclical history of criticism leveled at public schools in the United States (Cremin, 1977). Postman and Weingartner (1973) trace the beginning of one strand of criticism back to the 1930s, when decades of attacks were launched against John Dewey's progressive education for its alleged "gooey, precious, romantic philosophy, which stressed permissiveness and life adjustment" (p. 7).

By the late 1950s and early 1960s, new criticisms of public education emerged. Public schools were now under persistent attack for their failure to emphasize intellectual growth and rigorous thinking, especially after the Soviet launching of Sputnik I. Much of the criticism, originating in the business community, focused on the perceived need to eliminate "frills" from the public school curriculum (see Dougherty & Hammack, 1990). In the rhetoric of the cold war, the United States needed to train disciplined scientists and highly skilled technicians to regain its competitive edge over the Soviet Union. The business community argued that a "back-to-basics" educational approach was the solution (Campbell, Cunningham, Nystrand, & Usdan, 1985; Smith, 1990).

During the 1980s, the educational establishment produced a plethora of educational reform reports in response to the criticisms raised two decades earlier (e.g., National Commission on Excellence in Education, 1983; Education Commission of the States, 1983; Twentieth Century Fund Task Force on Federal Elementary and Secondary Education Policy, 1983). The reports' recommendations varied slightly, but they generally agreed that the conditions in public schools were indeed responsible for the U.S. decline in international economic competition. Ameliorative strategies such as school restructuring, site-based management, and teacher accountability quickly achieved a high profile across the country. The overarching goal of the strategies was to increase composite student achievement scores, thereby enhancing the country's ability to compete globally. In the rush to implement these reforms, the well-being of *individual* children was often overlooked (see Bastian, Fruchter, Gittel, Greer, & Haskins, 1985; Natriello, McDill, & Pallas, 1985).

Over the decades, the criticisms and contentions concerning public education spawned the growth of both private schools and home schools (Carper, 1983; Cooper, McLaughlin, & Manno, 1983). By the mid-1980s, parents started withdrawing their children from public schools at an unprecedented rate. Many parents chose to circumvent institutionalized forms of schooling by establishing home-based instructional programs for their children.

Confrontation

Prior to the confrontation phase, legitimate educational options were limited primarily to traditional private and parochial institutions. Other educational options, such as home schooling, occupied an obscure position. For example, although the limits of state regulation over private and parochial schools and the rights of parents to make educational choices for their children were delineated in four U.S. Supreme Court cases, the issue of home education was never directly addressed in any of the cases (Baker, 1988; Burgess, 1986; Knight, 1987; Stocklin-Enright, 1982; Tobak & Zirkel, 1982). Confrontations over home education emerged within this legal context.

The advent of the confrontation phase did not occur in isolation. Rather, it occurred in tandem with a national pattern of litigious and legislative action concerning a variety of educational issues. Between 1930 and 1970, for example, few changes were made in the laws governing the relationship between the rights of parents and the rights of states, relative to children's education (Vergon, 1986). After 1970, however, a number of significant state court and U.S. Supreme Court decisions were announced. The courts' decisions dealt both implicitly and explicitly with the rights of parents, the rights of states, and educational choice. It was in this era of burgeoning judicial activity that challenges to home education defined the confrontation phase.

Criticisms of home schools came relatively quickly during the 1970s as the public became more aware of their existence. Widespread litigious action followed and can be attributed in part to the distress administrators felt when suddenly confronted with multiple cases of parents who thought they could educate children better than the public schools (Ritter, 1979). In addition, judicial action was initiated in several states to resolve the conflicts that arose over the vagueness of statutes addressing the power of school administrators to monitor and regulate home education (Knight, 1987; Lupu, 1987; Smith & Klicka, 1987).

Confrontations in the Courts. Until 1972, three cases formed the constitutional backdrop for home education litigation—*Meyer v. Nebraska* (1923), *Pierce v. Society of Sisters* (1925), and *Farrington v. Tokushige* (1927). Each case dealt indirectly with Fourteenth Amendment due process rights regarding educational choice, although none of the petitioners in the cases were parents. Instead, the suits were filed by teachers and private school corporations who claimed that their rights to earn a living were denied as a result of improper regulation by the state. In each case, the U.S. Supreme Court agreed with the plaintiffs, ruling that the state could not so deprive them of their livelihood. Despite the fact that none of the cases addressed the Fourteenth Amendment due process rights of parents directly, parental rights to direct the education of their children were addressed in the holdings and dicta of all the cases.

This situation changed in 1972, however, when the U.S. Supreme Court heard the landmark case, *Wisconsin v. Yoder* and granted Amish parents the right to educate their children after the eighth grade. For the first time, the Court established parents' educational choice under both the due process clause of the Fourteenth Amendment and the free exercise clause of the First Amendment. The decision in the case was somewhat narrow, providing that to obtain Constitutional protection, "the parental interest must be religious in nature rather than philosophical or personal" (quoted in Tobak & Zirkel, 1982, p. 17). The Court also noted the state's strong interest in universal compulsory education but said, "it is by no means absolute to the exclusion or subordination of all other interests" (quoted in Tobak & Zirkel, 1982, p. 17).

The U.S. Supreme Court's ruling in *Wisconsin v. Yoder* (1972) was a radical departure from prevailing views regarding the relationship between the exercise of religious beliefs and compulsory education. The ruling, however, did not offer a definitive statement about who ultimately had the legal right to determine a child's educational destiny. Instead, the Court chose to leave that question unanswered amid vague and tenuous language. The balance between the fundamental religious freedom of the parents and the interest of the state was not legally defined.

The *Yoder* case proved a harbinger in litigation activity regarding parental rights to direct the education of their children. It sparked a flurry of court cases at the state level, most initiated by parents who operated home schools. The courts, however, rarely extend the decision of *Yoder* to parents who do not hold long-standing religious convictions (Richardson & Zirkel, 1991).[2]

Confrontations over compulsory attendance laws also marked this phase of the home school movement (see Richardson & Zirkel, 1991, for an extended discussion of these court cases). During the late 1970s, for example, an increasing number of parents attacked the compulsory attendance statutes on constitutional grounds (Tobak & Zirkel, 1982). The parents who initiated these cases attacked the statutes on the basis of the free exercise clause of the First and due process clause of the Fourteenth Amendment. Parents also engaged the Ninth Amendment, arguing that the education of children at home was a parental activity protected by their constitutional right to privacy.

Although most state courts refused to accept this line of argument, one notable exception was a 1978 Massachusetts case, *Perchemlides v. Frizzle,* in which the court allowed parents to choose from a full range of educational alternatives and held that independent learning programs need not be "equivalent" to public schools (King, 1983). In addition, the *Perchemlides* (1978) ruling supported Ninth Amendment claims stating that a parent's right to choose alternative forms of education was protected by their right to privacy. At a critical time in the growth of the home school movement, the *Perchemlides* (1978) ruling provided encouragement to home school parents. The defense attorney on the case remarked that the ruling was "the most explicit judicial direction so far given to a school superintendent and a school committee for dealing with requests for home schooling" (Bumstead, 1979, p. 97; see also Ritter, 1979).

During this period of contention, compulsory attendance laws were attacked on other grounds as well. For instance, most states had attendance laws stipulating that children must attend either public or private schools, but they did not allow home education as an alternative (Burgess, 1986). This prompted many parents to initiate lawsuits arguing that their home schools were equivalent to public or private schools. By the early 1980s, court decisions about this issue were about equally divided. In *Scoma v. Chicago Board of*

Education (1974), for example, home education was allowed but must be "commensurate with public school standards" to qualify as a private school (quoted in Tobak & Zirkel, 1982, p. 34). The North Carolina Court of Appeals took a similar view, ruling in *Delconte v. State* (1985) that home education complied with the state's compulsory attendance law; the ruling stated, "We do not agree that the legislature intended simply by use of the word 'school,' because of some intrinsic meaning invariably attached to the word, to preclude home instruction" (p. 646). The Supreme Court of Arkansas, however, took a different position in *Burrow v. State* (1984), ruling that the common understanding of a school means only institutional learning (see Knight, 1987, for a more detailed discussion of these cases; also see Richardson & Zirkel, 1991).

Finally, during the latter part of the confrontation phase, many home schooling parents initiated court cases that challenged compulsory attendance statutes on the grounds that they violated the Fourteenth Amendment because of vagueness and unlawful delegation of legislative power to school administrators (Knight, 1987; Lupu, 1987; Smith & Klicka, 1987). Courts in the states of Wisconsin, Georgia, and Ohio agreed with parents and ruled in their favor (Smith & Klicka, 1987). More recently, the decision in a 1987 Massachusetts Supreme Judicial Court case, *Care and Protection of Charles*, involved a compromise. The court ordered the parents and the school district to "resolve the matter by agreement" under judicial supervision, pursuant to procedural and substantive criteria that the court elaborated (quoted in Lupu, 1987, p. 972).

The latter part of the confrontation phase is marked also by an apparently declining frequency of court cases, although there are states that exhibit continued and even increased litigation. For example, issues relating to the "approval" of home schools by local school districts, the definition of home education, the monitoring of student progress and achievement, and the certification requirements of parent educators are eminent. A recent analysis of state court cases concluded that, "Although there have been some exceptions, the overall trend in recent years has been in favor of home instruction, making it an explicit [alternative] to compulsory institutional education under specific circumstances or criteria" (Richardson & Zirkel, 1991, p. 172). As this book was in preparation, the Michigan Supreme Court (*People v. DeJonge*, 1993) decided in a case that had been in litigation for 8 years, "to exempt families who home school due to their religious beliefs from the state requirement that students be taught by a state certified teacher" ("DeJonges Celebrate Victory," 1993, p. 1). The court decided that Michigan school officials failed to show that teacher certification was the least restrictive means of ensuring that children were educated. This may prove to be the most significant home education case in the past 20 years. Future cases, similar to the recent *People v. DeJonge* (1993), are bound to more fully explore issues regarding the policies and regulations that govern home schools.

Cooperation

Cooperation between public school officials and home school parents has not come easily. However, two factors help induce cooperation: Court cases generally favor parents (Ritter, 1979) and litigation is costly for school boards. The misgivings of a county attorney who testified before the education committee of the Minnesota House of Representatives illustrates this point:

> It costs us a lot of time and energy to take these cases through the courts; we get a lot of terrible publicity; we lose many more cases than we win; and even when we win we don't gain anything, for the family usually just moves to another school district, or perhaps out of state, and we or someone else has the whole thing to do all over again. (Merrill, 1983, p. 18)

Particularly since the mid-1980s, home school parents increasingly have sought to cooperate with school boards, principals, and teachers (Knowles, 1989). Obviously, cooperation is impossible when parents are forced into surreptitious home education. However, the recent changes in home school laws (often a result of the considerable legislative lobbying efforts of parent educators) have encouraged some degree of cooperation (Lines, 1985a).

During the height of the cooperation phase, state courts have provided specific directives limiting the actions school boards can take against home education parents, often advising them to explore avenues of cooperation (Bumstead, 1979; Ritter, 1979). In response, some school boards voluntarily have developed explicit policies of cooperation. The Granite School District in the greater Salt Lake City urban area is an example of one such district. The school district welcomes home schools to utilize the services of the public schools; home school students can use library materials and books, and enroll in special classes. Subject areas in which home-educated children typically enroll include science classes and music and art enrichment programs (Collin, 1983).

The San Diego (California) City School District serves as another model of cooperation between public schools and home education parents. There, the state of California funds a Community Home Education Program (CHE) that employs six teachers, each assigned about 34 students, 3 instructional aides, and a secretary. CHE is explicitly designed to serve as a liaison between home educators and public schools. The case study of CHE conducted by Dalaimo (in press) concluded that parents, children, and instructors formed close relationships that emphasized open communication, partnership, and teamwork. Moreover, Dalaimo (in press) found that by being part of CHE, parents had access to textbooks and services like testing, counseling, and special education and "enjoyed the security of being connected to the public school system."

On one level, cooperation was forced upon some school districts. On another level, however, cooperation occurred (and continues to occur) because forward-thinking educators recognize that home education is not a concept that can or should be defeated or ignored. It is likely that more cooperative programs will be developed as home education becomes more visible and acceptable to the general public (Knowles, 1989). The models presented above suggest just a couple of the ways cooperation between public schools and home schools can occur—an issue we discuss in more detail in Chapters 5 and 7.

Consolidation

During the 1970s and early 1980s, home school parents frequently perceived themselves as ideologically alienated from the larger educational community. Their quest for anonymity often meant that they were also separated from other parent educators. In addition, the proliferation of court cases frequently isolated home school families from friends, neighbors, and the public at large. The publicity associated with home school litigation, however, aided home education parents in forging bonds with other known sympathetic parent educators. As a result, home school parents began to network.

Networking is now widespread, particularly among religiously motivated home school families, and is probably the single most important factor in the continued consolidation of the home education movement. The consolidation phase, however, is best understood as the result of a combination of the following circumstances: (a) the growing public acceptance of home education, especially as reflected in media coverage; (b) the prolonged and perplexing problems facing public schools, commonly defined as the "crisis in education"; (c) the networking achievements of parent educators at the local, state, and national levels by way of grassroots publications and home school organizations; (d) the publication of a relatively extensive number of home school "how to" books and curricular materials, both commercially and by entrepreneurs who are themselves parent educators; and (e) the availability of correspondence programs and courses, particularly those aimed at the home school market. In addition, some aspects of consolidation have been tied to the growth of the religious right during the past decade. By 1990, the growth of home education was no longer attributable to liberal educational reformers and proselytizers. Instead, conservative religious parents made up a majority of the home school population and provided the impulse behind many of the networking efforts.

As a result of these circumstances, the home school movement has accelerated toward consolidation of its very disparate groups and practitioners. In the next two sections of this chapter, we explore these developments in more detail.

Media Coverage: From Menaces to Heroes. During the 1970s, the mass media helped shape public attitudes toward home education, often portraying parent educators and their home schools in a disparaging light. An examination of over 60 mass media articles about home schools gleaned from major newspapers throughout the

United States reveals that in the 9 years from 1970 to 1979, the primary focus of the articles was on the most divisive and extreme home education court cases and their outcomes. Furthermore, home school parents were often portrayed as neglectful and irresponsible (Stevens, 1979). In recent years, however, home schools have been viewed in a more positive light. Many supportive articles now appear in weekly news magazines, national newspapers, popular monthly magazines, and professional journals (see, e.g., Avner, 1989; Churbuck, 1993; Holt, 1984; Kohn, 1988; Roach, 1989; Rowe, 1987; Seligmann & Abramson, 1988; Toch et al., 1991).

The noticeable change in the media's portrayal of home schooling began about the time of *Perchemlides* decision in 1978. From 1979 to 1983, for instance, newspaper and magazine articles commonly noted the benefits of home education. In one case, the success of Grant Colfax and his younger brothers, who received their education at home before distinguishing themselves at Harvard University, received national media attention (see Colfax & Colfax, 1988). The more successful cooperative efforts of home school parents and professional educators also appeared with increasing regularity. Furthermore, court cases generally were presented in a less disparaging way than those reported during the early years of the movement.

During the 1980s and early 1990s, the media's broadening coverage emphasized the growth and popularity of home schools, sometimes portraying parent educators as folk heroes. For example, a *New York Times* article described 14-year-old Cara Tanstrom's struggle to participate in the North Dakota state spelling bee: "State education officials had tried to block Cara and other children who are taught in their homes from participation in the contest, but they backed down after national publicity and pressure from the Scripps-Howard National Spelling Bee, which said the contest should be open to any student" ("Victories for Home Schooling," 1989, p. 26).[3] Similarly, a recent *Los Angeles Times* article showcased four successful home education families who described the educational benefits their children received by being schooled at home ("Home Schooling: The Best Education," 1992).

Networks, Networking, and Gurus. Consolidation also meant that the number of networking organizations available to home school parents grew rapidly. In the early years of the movement, many parent educators operated their home schools in isolation. The proliferation of court cases discussed earlier had the effect of isolating many home school families from their friends, neighbors, and local educational communities. Home school parents, however, responded to their isolation by forming networks and organizing home school support groups in an attempt to forge bonds with other known sympathetic home educating families.

Throughout the 1980s, the number of networking organizations grew and served (and continue to serve) home education parents socially, ideologically, and politically. Parent educators quickly recognized that the social and curricular support provided by local and statewide networks was an essential element of operating a home school (Bates, 1991; Bishop, 1991; Gustavsen, 1981; Van Galen, 1986). Their involvement in networking organizations created a situation wherein they were exposed to the inspiration of other parents who taught their children at home. Furthermore, in their search for curricular materials, teaching methods, and legal information, they met similar-minded people with which to share their experiences (Bishop, 1991).

Home school organizations functioned (and continue to function) for parent educators in other ways as well. Parents joined organizations whose participants held interests, values, and beliefs similar to their own. Not only did these associations help unify similarly motivated groups of parent educators (e.g., religious or secular), but they supported the particular meanings parents gave to the act of home educating their children (Hadeed, 1991). For example, secular home education organizations typically focused on issues regarding (a) pedagogical approaches that differed from those in mainstream conventional schools; (b) the individual intellectual, social, and psychological needs of children; (c) supporting and encouraging parent educators, and (d) influencing legislators and other policy makers. Christian home education organizations, however, explained that home education was based on the principles of the scriptures and was the best educational approach for raising children to be mature in the beliefs of Christianity. Christian organizations also engaged in many of the same activities and shared some of the goals of the secular groups. They advocated various pedagogical approaches, supported one another in small meetings and large conferences, and lobbied their legislators and other policy makers. Consequently, participation in networks and home school organizations provided parent educators with a discourse that both supported their choice to educate their children at home and legitimated the reasons they had for making that choice.

Networking now occurs at the local, state, national, and international levels. At the local level, families interact with fellow home educators, providing mutual support and encouragement, and often sharing their home instruction resources with each other. Local networks are often formed by parents who share strong religious, ideological, and pedagogical beliefs (Hadeed, 1991).

At the state level, more extensive opportunities for networking exist. Similar to local networks, statewide organizations are distinguished by their religious, ideological and pedagogical orientations (Hadeed, 1991). For example, the Utah Home Education Association (UHEA) was formed in the early 1980s to provide curricular and instructional support to home school parents throughout the state. In the mid-1980s, however, the Utah Christian Home School Association (UCHSA) splintered off from UHEA as a result of ideological divisions. UCHSA was formed in response to what its president called the "humanistic perspectives" of UHEA. Essentially formed as a group of evangelical (and non-Mormon) Christian parents, UCHSA's membership networks by way of regular meetings, workshops, and seminars. To date, UHEA is more tightly unified than UCHSA, primarily due to the coherence of its members' religious perspectives and lifestyles.

Family Centered Learning Alternatives (FCLA) is another example of a state networking organization. FCLA originated in the state of Washington in response to state laws that required home schools to be classified under the umbrella of private schools. Now established in a number of states across the country, FCLA brings together groups of parents with similar pedagogical orientations. With the assistance of parent educators, FCLA produces educational materials and facilitates other cooperative activities for parent educators and their children, such as workshops and field trips.

At the national level, the National Center for Home Education (NCHE) and the National Homeschool Association (NHA) provide information and support services to statewide and local home education support groups. NCHE's strongest, although not exclusive, connection is with Christian and politically conservative home school parents. Among other things, NCHE has established a congressional action program to lobby members of Congress, both on Capitol Hill and in their home districts. NCHE also operates a facsimile alert system to contact statewide organizations across the nation and then disseminate the information to local support groups and individual families. In addition, NCHE serves as a clearinghouse on issues of home education policy and research. NHA, similar in some ways to NCHE, works more closely with secular parent educators who are more interested in home education as a single issue rather than as linked to other political and religious concerns.

Several publications are very influential at the national level. *The Teaching Home* (*TTH*), owned and operated by one family since its founding in 1980, grew from a local newsletter to a 70-plus-page bimonthly magazine with about 40,000 paid subscribers. *TTH* serves home school families in all 50 states and 81 foreign countries, featuring practical tips on how to home educate, legal news and advice, research reports, and special reports on topics such as teaching science at home and home schooling teenagers. *TTH* has a distinct and forthright Christian intent. *Home Education Magazine* is also a family-produced periodical that is an example of the "do-it-yourself" efforts of home educating families. Disseminated across the country, *HEM* provides parent educators with examples of specific teaching and learning activities that can be incorporated into their home instruction programs.

The publications of Raymond Moore and the late John Holt also have had a considerable impact on the consolidation of the home school movement at the national level. *Growing Without Schooling* (*GWS*), a bimonthly magazine, was founded by Holt in 1977. Subscription sales now exceed 5,000 and the magazine reflects the networking phenomenon of home education. A directory of consenting home school families is regularly updated and published in each issue. *GWS* also reports up-to-date legal information regarding home education and provides a listing of "helpful schools," "friendly lawyers," "professors and other allies," "correspondence schools," and "home schooling organizations." Moore's publication, *Moore*

Report International, resemble *GWS* in intent, but it primarily serves
Christian home school families. This publication is not, however,
excessively Christian in flavor. Rather, it has an underlying theme
of holistic family participation in the education process and pro-
motes certain early childhood education practices. Other periodicals
that reach national audiences are *Home School Court Report, Practical
Home Schooling, Homeschooling Today, Home School Digest,* and *Christian Home Education News.*

Consolidation at the national level has been further facilitated by
other individuals and groups involved in networking activities. For
example, Gregg Harris, director of Christian Life Workshops, conducts workshops around the country. His workshops teach parents
basic and advanced aspects of home education. His workshops also
assist churches and Christian home education groups in establishing support organizations for parent educators. Nationwide
correspondence schools, such as the Clonlara Home Based Education program in Michigan, Calvert in Maryland, A Beka in Florida,
Christian Liberty Academy in Illinois, and others, assist home-
educated children and their parents by providing curricular information and networking opportunities (see Lines, 1991a).

Consolidation at the international level also has occurred primarily because of the wide dissemination of publications such as *Growing Without Schooling* and *The Teaching Home* to subscribers on all
continents. The Home School Legal Defense Association (HSLDA)
defends parents' rights to educate their children at home. HSLDA
maintains about 38,000 active members in all 50 states and numerous
foreign countries. The prevalence of internationally publicized home
education conferences also have assisted the consolidation process.
Books by home education advocates like Michael Farris, Gregg Harris,
John Holt, Christopher Klicka, and Raymond Moore are now internationally available to practicing and potential parent educators.

Parent educators' increasing participation in a growing number
of home school organizations and networks, such as those mentioned above, supports Hadeed's (1991) contention that "what began as a relatively private endeavor on the part of a small number
of parents has taken on a progressively more public character . . .
and assumed the form and structure of an organized collective
action" (p. 1). It is likely that the number of home schools will

continue to grow and consolidate their position as bona fide educational institutions.

Compartmentalization

The consolidation phase has led directly to a settling and shifting period in the home school movement. Unlike the consolidation phase, which clearly has fortified the lobbying clout of home school parents, the outcomes of the compartmentalization phase are still unclear. The increasing number and diversity of home school organizations may potentially dilute parent educators' political power or bring new strength to the larger home school community.

The compartmentalization phase in part has paralleled the activities and circumstances evident in the consolidation phase. The networking organizations that have made possible the productive connections between home school families also have offered them the chance to fine-tune their educational philosophies. Consequently, the membership of various networking organizations have become increasingly homogenous. Holt Associates, for example, serves primarily liberal, secular, and humanistic home education families. The most recent (and increasingly powerful) additions to the networking arena, however, are conservative and Christian parent educators. The distinctive educational philosophies and beliefs held by members of these particular networks result at times in fractionalizing the home school community. A parent educator in Nevada made this point when asked about her affiliation with home school organizations:

> This has been kind of a stumbling block because most of the organizations [in Las Vegas, Nevada] are more religious. I am ostracized or shunned because of my lack of theological conviction. I remember at one of the organization meetings, it came up that I was an atheist. You would have thought I grew horns and goat eyes. It just freaked some people out. People were scared of that.

The compartmentalization phase is further exacerbated by the growth of networking organizations that publish and sell home education books, magazines, curricula materials, and correspondence courses. These developments in the movement have made visible the considerable time and money invested in home education. The livelihood of many individuals is dependent on generating financial support through the sales of their wares to home school families living in particular locales and regions, possessing definite religious, political, and educational philosophies.

The gradual rise of the conservative right, religious voice has further compartmentalized the movement. After coming together with families of more liberal perspectives to respond to legislative issues during the 1980s, conservative home school parents are now strongly making their differences known. For example, during the 1980s, the Wisconsin Parent Association (WPA) held a conference offering workshops on how to teach academic subjects and providing other information to home education parents. One Christian leader went away from the WPA conference "feeling empty and thinking there was more to home education" than what she had experienced (J. Gnacinski, personal communication to B. Ray, May 17, 1994). She and her husband later experienced great joy while attending a Christian seminar that dealt with home education, child discipline, peer interaction for youth, and other topics. As a result of prayer they believed that they were called to start a distinctively Christian statewide organization in Wisconsin and did so by early 1991. The rapid growth of their organization, the Wisconsin Christian Home Educators Association, was evidenced by the fact that the 1994 conference was attended by about 940 adults. As we write, considerable debates are occurring in the home school community about such matters.

The compartmentalization phase is thus characterized by events that at first may seem destructively divisive but may ultimately prove to have advantages for the movement. Leaders who do not sustain productive, focused perspectives may be weeded out. Some network leaders, particularly those with commercial interests, may encourage their membership and clientele to be nonpartisan in their allegiance to particular educational and religious points of view. Despite the eventual outcome of the compartmentalization phase, however, home educating parents and their leaders continue to effectively muster significant unified strength for lobbying legislators, influencing policy makers, and winning court battles.[4] The most fundamental issue, perhaps, is that parent educators hold in common their commitment to the teaching of, and love for, their children.

Conclusion

The five phases of the home school movement are by no means definitive or complete. Contentions about public schools, confrontations with public school administrators over the laws and policies that regulate home schools, cooperation with public schools, and the consolidation and compartmentalization of the home education movement are all readily apparent in the movement today. Parents' problems with public schools persist; the courts are still dealing with legal issues regarding home education; cooperative home school-public school programs continue to spring up around the country; home school organizations and networks remain central to the consolidation of the movement and the continued operation of home schools; and compartmentalization continues as promoters of particular ideologies seek the affirmation and allegiance of home education parents.

The significance of the home education movement to the future development of home school policy is not yet clear. As home schools gain legitimacy and credibility, it is likely that regulations pertaining to home education will need further refinement and explication. It is also likely that an increasing number of school districts will develop public school-home school cooperative programs. As policy makers struggle with these issues, questions will arise concerning the goals, expectations, and aspirations of the various factions making up the home school movement. What regulations governing home schools will parent educators of various persuasions accept? What resources will religious parent educators desire from cooperative programs? What resources will other parent educators expect? Can home school policies and cooperative programs treat parent educators fairly and equally? These questions are increasingly important as the growth of the home education movement continues at an unprecedented rate. We will return to them in Chapters 5 and 7.

Notes

1. Over the last 10 years, many of our colleagues in education and other disciplines have viewed home education as an aberrant educational activity, a "fad," soon to move out of the educational arena. We doubt this to be the case.

2. A recent U.S. Supreme Court decision, *Employment Division, Department of Human Resources of Oregon et al. v. Smith et al.* (1990), prohibited the use of peyote for religious purposes and established a new standard in "free exercise of religion" cases. Previously, the state had been required to justify its infringement on the free exercise of religion by providing a compelling justification of government interest. As a result of the *Smith* decision, however, the state was relieved of its burden to justify the denial of free exercise, if the practice of religion involved a breach of criminal laws. Without this compelling interest test, it was highly unlikely that parents who violated state compulsory attendance or certification laws could successfully argue their cases on the basis of First Amendment free exercise protection. This was all apparently changed, however, when President Clinton signed into law the Religious Freedom Restoration Act (RFRA) of 1993. RFRA, in essence, restored the compelling state interest test. A few weeks after RFRA was made law, Home School Legal Defense Association (HSLDA) attorneys "found it helpful in advancing religious freedom claims," and one HSLDA attorney "cited the RFRA in an important Virginia home school case" (*Home School Court Report*, 1993, p. 11).

3. Copyright © 1989 by *The New York Times* Company. Reprinted by permission.

4. An excellent example of this effective lobbying occurred as this book was going to press. Many home educators concluded that as of early 1994 there was wording in U.S. House of Representatives Resolution 6 (H.R. 6) that could be construed as requiring all home educators to be government-certified teachers. Although there were some differences among home educators about how the language should be amended, they were unified in believing that something needed to be done. Home educators who supported two different approaches worked together quickly and effectively, made headlines in major newspapers and other news media around the nation, and succeeded in getting their voices heard on Capitol Hill. The first, simpler amendment was passed with an astonishing vote of 424 to 1. The second, more comprehensive and protective amendment was later passed by an equally remarkable vote of 374 to 53.

3

Parents Who Teach Their Children at Home

A substantial majority of home schooling parents in America are fervently religious and view schools as at odds with Christian doctrine. Overall, however, they are a diverse lot—the orthodox and the progressive, the Fundamentalist Christian and the libertarian, the urban, the rural, the social skeptic, the idealist, the self-sufficient, and the paranoid.

—David Guterson (1990, p. 59)[1]

In Chapter 2, we discussed the growth and development of the home education movement. In this and the following chapter, we ask pertinent questions about the parents who establish home schools. Who are these parents and why did they choose to educate their children at home? What experiences led them to consider home education? Why is teaching one's children at home a meaningful experience for parent educators? We examine the characteristics, experiences, and thinking of home-educating parents in Nevada, Washington, and Utah. We analyze their differences and commonalities to gain a better understanding of what makes home schooling an appealing educational alternative to such a wide range of parents.

We begin our analysis with the demographic, religious, and political characteristics of the parents who operate home schools. Our account illustrates not only the commonalities among home school parents, but the diversity among them as well. Although the discussion draws from a nonrepresentative sample of parent educators in Washington, Nevada, and Utah, great care was taken to represent the multiple subpopulations of the home school movement (see Chapter 1). Bear in mind also that this study (and virtually all studies of home school parents) primarily represents heterosexual, white, nuclear families. We acknowledge that home schools are operated by people of color, single parents, gay and lesbian parents, and parents living in intentional communities. The number of parent educators from these groups, however, is small; they are, therefore, less likely to be represented in research reports.

Home-Educating Parents: Some Characteristics

Demographic Characteristics

Table 3.1 shows that home education is clearly the domain of a largely white population (98%) and not common among African American, Hispanic, American Indian, Asian American, or other racial and ethnic groups. We are personally aware of a small number of families from these groups who operate home schools, but such families are difficult to locate and appear hesitant to join the European American-dominated networking organizations through which our subjects were located. Table 3.1 also demonstrates that the majority of parents (60%) who operate home schools are relatively "young" (in their 30s). Not surprising, given the pressures associated with providing a family income and teaching children at home, most are married (97%) and very few are divorced, widowed, or never married.

Table 3.2 illustrates that parent educators, compared to state populations in Washington, Utah, and Nevada, received significantly more formal education than did their state counterparts.[2] Almost one half (43%) of the home education parents that we surveyed attended college or a trade school, and one third (33%) graduated

TABLE 3.1 Race and Ethnicity, Age, and
          Marital Status of Home
          Educators (in percentages)

Race/Ethnicity	
white	98
African American	<1
Hispanic	<1
American Indian	<1
Asian American	1
other	<1
Age	
under 30	7
30-39	60
40 and above	32
Marital Status	
married	97
divorced	2
widowed	<1
never married	<1

NOTE: Totals may not equal 100 due to rounding.

from college with an undergraduate degree. Compared to state populations, a significantly larger percentage of parent educators received a graduate degree of some kind.[3] Interestingly, a small percentage (10%) of parent educators did not receive any post-high school education, but they still chose to take primary responsibility for their children's education. This situation may seem surprising, yet research studies fail to find any significant relationship between home-educated children's achievement scores and parental educational attainment (Havens, 1991; Ray, 1990c; Ray & Wartes, 1991).

The occupational distribution of home-educating parents that we studied is also significantly different from statewide populations (see Table 3.2). Parent educators are more likely to be employed in professional or technical jobs and less likely to work in sales, clerical, service, craft, and semiskilled or unskilled occupations. Home-educating fathers' written responses to the survey indicate that

TABLE 3.2 Education and Occupation of Home Educators
Compared to State Populations in Washington, Utah,
and Nevada (in percentages)

Level of Education/ Occupational Category	Home Educators	State Residents[a]	Chi-Square Statistic
Educational Attainment			
less than 4 years high school	2	18	408.9*
high school graduate	10	29	351.8*
some college or trade school	43	35	61.5*
college graduate	33	14	827.5*
completed graduate education	12	8	181.2*
Occupation			
professional/technical	31	13	767.3*
managerial/administrative	10	19	116.8*
sales/clerical	4	28	689.1*
craft and kindred	4	12	162.7*
semiskilled/unskilled	3	13	219.4*
service	4	12	174.9*
farm/ranch	2	3	4.8
homemaker/home educator	40[b]	NA	NA
not part of labor force	3	NA	NA

NOTES: Totals may not equal 100 due to rounding.
a. The source for this column is U.S. Bureau of the Census (1990, CP-2-30, pp. 51, 53; CP-2-49, pp. 65, 87; CP-2-46, pp. 62, 65).
b. 78% of home education mothers marked this category.
*$p < .01$.

many hold positions in small, privately owned firms offering them a high degree of work time flexibility (e.g., small business owner, independent sales, private contractor).

The results of previous studies demonstrated that the tasks associated with running home-based education programs were almost always carried out by mothers not employed in the paid labor force (Gladin, 1987; Mayberry, 1988; Wartes, 1988). Our study supports that finding: 63% of the mothers that we surveyed are responsible for 90% or more of the day-to-day operation of the home school.

Thus it was not surprising to find that over three quarters (78%) of the mothers listed their occupation as "homemaker/home educator" (see Table 3.2). Nearly all of the mothers who listed an occupation other than "homemaker/home educator" (e.g., bookkeeping for family business, catering service, child care, craftsmaker) mentioned that they conduct their work activities in the home, thereby finding time to organize the learning activities of their children.

Given the preponderance of mothers who listed their occupation as "homemaker/home educator," we wondered why families relinquish the chance to obtain additional income in order to teach their children at home. Written responses to our survey suggest that many mothers perceived the job of home teaching as "more important" than the additional income they would gain from paid employment. Indeed, the enhancement of the family's economic status and financial security is often viewed by parent educators as secondary to the learning and socialization activities that occur in the home school. One mother we interviewed described her commitment to providing for her children's education by saying: "I am highly invested emotionally in their well-being and am motivated by love, not by financial status." Her statement reflects the sentiment that many home educators expressed during our interviews with them.

Finally, home education is primarily a middle-class activity (see Table 3.3). Parent educators in general, compared to state populations, are financially better off. Over one half (57%) of the home education families earn $25,000 to $50,000 a year, whereas only 37% percent of the state residents achieve yearly incomes in that range. The one exception is the larger percentage of state residents who earn more than $50,000 yearly. We suspect that there are two reasons for this: the likelihood that parent educators are employed by small, privately owned firms and the probability that many support their family on a single income. Families with limited financial resources also conduct home-based educational programs; 15% of the parents that we surveyed operate home schools on what the U.S. government generally considers a "lower" income, that is, below $20,000 yearly (U.S. Bureau of the Census, 1993).

TABLE 3.3 Income of Home Education Families Compared
to State Populations in Washington, Utah, and
Nevada (in percentages)

Family Income	Home Educators	State Residents[a]	Chi-Square Statistic
Less than $10,000	3	13	107.6*
$10,000-$14,999	4	9	29.1*
$15,000-$19,999	8	9	3.4
$20,000-$24,999	11	9	6.7
$25,000-$34,999	31	17	167.7*
$35,000-$49,999	26	20	32.5*
More than $50,000	16	23	33.4*

NOTES: Totals may not equal 100 due to rounding.
a. The source for this column is U.S. Bureau of the Census (1990, CP-2-30, p. 46; CP-2-49, p. 82; CP-2-46, p. 57).
*$p < .01$.

Clearly, the home education movement draws primarily from the young, well-educated, and middle-income segments of society. Yet, the demographic characteristics of parent educators are not monolithic; parents with less education and fewer financial resources are also teaching their children at home. In many ways, home schooling is an educational choice that appeals to a wide spectrum of people. We suspect, however, that parents who are better situated than others to home school have flexible work situations, stable family incomes, and high levels of education. In turn, these families are more likely to transform their ambitions into realities.

Religious Characteristics

The religiosity of home school families is particularly striking and noted in many research reports (Gladin, 1987; Mayberry, 1988; Wartes, 1988). Table 3.4 compares the level of church attendance and religious commitment of the parent educators who participated in this study with the National Opinion Research Center (NORC) sample of the national population. Compared to the national population,

TABLE 3.4 Church Attendance and Religious Commitment of
Home Educators Compared to a Sample of the
National Population (in percentages)

Religiosity	*Home Educators*	*NORC*[a]	*Chi-Square Statistic*
Church Attendance			
weekly/several times weekly	78	30	337.3*
2-3 times monthly/			
nearly weekly	11	15	12.8*
less than once a year/			
once a month	11	55	709.8*
Importance of Religious Commitment			
very important	91	40	295.9*
somewhat important	5	15	102.3*
not very important	2	45	1,089.4*
not important at all	1	NA	NA

NOTES: Totals may not equal 100 due to rounding.
a. The source for this column is NORC (1990).
*$p < .01$.

parent educators are clearly more religiously oriented. For instance,
more than three quarters (78%) of the home education parents that
we surveyed attend church at least once a week, whereas less than
one third (30%) of the national population attend church as often.
Church attendance among the national population is significantly
less frequent. Furthermore, the vast majority (91%) of home school
parents feel strongly committed to their religion, indicating that
their religious commitment is "very important." The national population views their religious commitment as significantly less important. In fact, nearly one half (45%) of the national sample rank their
religious commitment as "not very important."

In addition, we discovered that the majority of parent educators
were raised in "mainstream" religious institutions (e.g., Methodist,
Episcopalian, Presbyterian). However, many became members of
Evangelical religious organizations in their adult years and now practice those religions in the family setting. For instance, approximately

one third of the parent educators in our sample belong to Evangelical, Pentecostal, and other "nondenominational" religious organizations, whereas slightly less than one quarter are affiliated with "mainstream" religious organizations. Twenty-five percent of the parent educators whom we surveyed belong to the Church of Latter Day Saints. This percentage is not unexpected as Utahan home school families were included in our study. Previous research has not identified any significant number of Mormon home school families in other states.

Table 3.5 demonstrates that the vast majority of parent educators that we surveyed express strong agreement with each item included on a scale of Christian religious orthodoxy. This response is not surprising given the orthodox doctrinal orientation of the religious organizations to which many of these families belong. The home-educating parents who agree with the statements that measure religious orthodoxy believe in the existence of an *external* authority, an authority that guides their moral decisions, including the decision to educate their children at home. For instance, during interviews many religious parent educators referred to Deuteronomy to explain why they chose home education:

> And these words, which I am commanding you today, shall be on your heart; and you shall teach them diligently to your sons and shall talk of them when you sit in your house and when you walk by the way and when you lie down and when you rise up. (Deuteronomy 6:6, 7, New American Standard translation)

Not all parent educators, however, subscribe to orthodox religious beliefs (see Table 3.5). A small percentage of them either "strongly disagreed" or "disagreed" with the items on the scale of religious orthodoxy. Although some of these parents did not indicate why they disagreed with the items, others wrote comments on the survey describing their affiliation with a "new spirituality" commonly known as New Age philosophy (see, Beckford, 1984; Hannigan, 1988; Hargrove, 1988). Unlike Christian parent educators, these parents believe in the *internal* nature of authority; that is, for them, the ultimate source of authority resides within the individual, not

TABLE 3.5 Religious Orthodoxy of Home Educators (in percentages)

Item	Strongly Agree	Agree	Uncertain	Disagree	Strongly Disagree
Believe Bible is inspired word of God and literally true	68	16	2	8	6
Believe in such places as heaven and hell	79	12	2	3	4
Eternal life is gift of God to those who believe in Jesus Christ	73	8	2	7	10
Satan is working in the world today	86	7	1	2	4
God lives and is real	93	4	1	1	1

SOURCE: Reprinted with permission from Shupe, A., & Stacey, W. (1983). In Liebman, Robert C. and Robert Wuthnow. *The New Christian Right* (p. 115). New York: Aldine de Gruyter. Copyright © 1983 Robert C. Liebman and Robert Wuthnow.
NOTE: Totals may not equal 100 due to rounding.

with God. This belief informed both their philosophy of education and their decision to home educate their children. During interviews, several parents who were aligned with New Age philosophy remarked that education should address all interrelated aspects of the *human* experience—emotional, spiritual, intuitive, creative, aesthetic, and rational. The place where such an education could occur, they stressed, is in the home.

The range of religious and spiritual orientations exhibited by parent educators reveals much about the ideological diversity within the home school movement. For instance, one father from the Evangelical faith recounted in an interview his rationale for operating a home school:

It is based on the fact that God gave parents, not the state, the responsibility to educate children. We [parents] alone must answer for their upbringing. Morals, spiritual growth, and God-centered living are the central focus for a proper education, and public schools are unable to teach that. Humanism is the core of public instruction, and it leads to societal decay.

In contrast, one mother, an advocate of New Age spirituality, feels that home instruction offers her the chance to teach her children the secular and humanistic concepts of New Age philosophy; these are, ironically, the concepts that many Christian parent educators want to shield their children from. During an interview, this mother described her educational philosophy in the following way:

> We do not believe in Christianity. We study many New Age concepts that help us understand all people as [being] equal, that stop religious and cultural belittlement of women, that respect Mother Earth and animals. And we teach the real truth about American history and not a "God's on our side and we can't do anything wrong" slanted viewpoint. Public schools don't encourage freedom of thought. It's important to us that our kids be exposed to all ideas. It's equally important to us that they learn how to process that information. When we discuss things, I try to present all sides of an issue and then we discuss it thoroughly. I may state my position, as well as others, but they generally draw their own conclusions. It's the kind of thinking process that's difficult for kids to get in the public [school] system. We teach them to resolve their needs. If push came to shove, they could perish waiting for a resolution outside of themselves.

Not all parent educators, however, operate home schools to instill in their children particular sets of religious or spiritual values. Twenty percent of the parents we studied did not indicate a religious affiliation, and 12% did not respond to the scale of religious orthodoxy. The written comments of these parent educators indicate that teaching their children particular religious and spiritual values is not the primary motivating factor in their decision to operate a home school. Rather, their primary goal for home instruction is to provide their children with an effective learning environment. During an interview, one mother made the significance of this goal apparent:

> We are not a religious family. But my children were entrusted to me and it is my responsibility to see that they grow to be conscientious, responsible, and intelligent people. This is too important of a job to be given to someone I don't even know.

The different rationales that parents have for home instruction are obvious. The underlying commonality between them, however, is less apparent. In each instance, home schooling provides parents the opportunity to expand personal and family rights, regardless of their secular or religious orientations. Looked at in this way, the growth of the home school movement represents the attempt of a widely diverse group of parents to decide how their children will be educated, what values they will learn, and which socialization experiences they will encounter. A narrower conceptualization of the motivations behind parents' decision to teach their children at home misses this point and reduces home education to an ideologically bound activity.

Political Characteristics

Table 3.6 reveals some interesting results with respect to home-educating parents' political characteristics. Most notably, the political affiliations and viewpoints of the parent educators who participated in this study differ significantly from a sample of the national population (NORC, 1990). More than three quarters (76%) of the home-educating parents are affiliated with the Republican party; conversely, only 7% indicate any tie to the Democratic party. In the national sample of the population, however, the Republican and Democratic parties are endorsed by a nearly equal number of people.

The majority of home school parents label their political views as "conservative" or "extremely conservative" (77%), whereas only 19% of the national sample share these two similar political viewpoints. It is also interesting to note the very small percentage of parent

TABLE 3.6 Political Affiliation and Viewpoint of Home
Educators Compared to a Sample of the National
Population (in percentages)

Political Orientation	Home Educators	NORC[a]	Chi-Square Statistic
Political Affiliation			
strong Democrat	1	12	137.9*
not very strong Democrat	3	23	231.8*
Independent, close to Democrat	3	10	45.9*
Independent	10	12	2.0
Independent, close to Republican	27	10	99.7*
strong Republican	31	12	20.9*
not very strong Republican	18	20	29.3*
other party	7	1	70.3*
Political Viewpoint			
extremely liberal	<1	3	11.6
liberal	3	11	65.9*
slightly liberal	3	14	100.0*
moderate, middle of the road	7	36	269.1*
slightly conservative	10	18	31.8*
conservative	59	15	351.8*
extremely conservative	18	4	120.7*

NOTES: Totals may not equal 100 due to rounding.
a. The source for this column is NORC (1990).
*$p < .01$.

educators who hold either "moderate" (7%) or liberal (6%) political viewpoints. In contrast, over one half (64%) of the national population label themselves either politically moderate or liberal.

Finally, we found that home school parents, as a group, have little confidence in a range of social institutions. This trend is not apparent in the national population (NORC, 1990). Parent educators have little confidence in banks and financial institutions, major companies, public education, the executive branch of the government, organized labor, the press, or the U.S. Supreme Court. It is noteworthy, however, given the large number of parent educators who align themselves with the Republican party and who maintain conservative political viewpoints, that institutions commonly thought of as conservative in orientation (e.g., the U.S. Supreme Court, organized religion, and the military) are also suspect among this group.

Thus many home school parents view large-scale social institutions with a great degree of skepticism. Previous research on this topic (Mayberry, 1988, 1989), combined with the findings of our study, suggest that this skepticism did not develop with the onset of the home school; rather, distrust of large-scale social institutions has been an ongoing feature of these persons' adult life. It is likely, therefore, that the decision many parents made to circumvent public institutions of education fits well with previously established personal beliefs. Indeed, many of the parent educators we studied find home schooling to be one way of maintaining the autonomy of the family unit in the face of institutional intrusion and regulation (see also Mayberry, 1988; Mayberry & Knowles 1989). One mother, who home schools her daughter for what she felt were the academic benefits, articulated this point during an interview:

> I feel every parent has the right and obligation to choose how this child will be taught. It's one of those natural, God-given rights that the Bill of Rights talks about. . . . The government has no right to supervise nor make requirements on any family. We all have different needs, desires, and interests. . . . The government is the servant of the people. As it is, the government is becoming like a king and people like subjects to it.

We were intrigued by the degree of skepticism that parent educators expressed about large-scale social institutions. Consequently, we wondered what they thought about the government's funding of public education. We predicted, based upon parent educators' strong desire for autonomy from external agencies, that any support for government financing would be negligible. Surprisingly, we found a lack of consensus about this issue; 37% of the parent educators we studied indicated that "too little" money is being spent on public education, whereas 45% felt that "too much" is being spent.

The extensive interviews that we conducted revealed two distinctive orientations regarding public school financing. One orientation was expressed by parents who are convinced of the academic, social, and moral superiority of home-based education. These parents have little use for public schools and state that they would continue to educate their children at home regardless of how well public schools are funded or what quality of education they offer. The parents who hold these convictions see little benefit to increasing expenditures for public education, especially as the new revenues would be generated by increasing personal taxes.

Another orientation toward public school financing was made clear by parents who decide about continuing their home school program on a "year-by-year" basis. These parents, willing to take advantage of public school facilities and services when offered, indicate that their children's future enrollment in public school is a possibility. In turn, these parents expressed volition to support the increased financing of public education. As one mother explained during the course of an interview:

> If we're allowed and encouraged access to public school facilities and programs, then I feel all citizens should be financially supporting public schools and working to improve them.

Thus the question of public education financing is viewed by parent educators from diverse vantage points. Families who desire full autonomy from public schools resist current tax policies to fund public education. In contrast, families who have some use for the programs and facilities offered by public schools support government funding of public education. The significance of these positions for school administrators and policy makers will be discussed in greater detail in Chapters 5 and 7.

What Should We Remember?

Certain trends in the home school population that we studied can be identified. First, it seems clear that home education is generally a white, middle-class movement, chosen primarily by relatively young parents living in traditional nuclear families. These parents tend to be generally well-educated, and the fathers are often employed in work situations that offer them a large degree of work time flexibility and autonomy. Second, the religious and spiritual convictions of many parent educators are a prominent feature of their daily lives. Consequently, their decision to operate a home school was often directly related to the religious and spiritual philosophies that organize other aspects of their lives. Third, home-educating parents are for the most part politically conservative and affiliated with the Republican party. Finally, these parents have little confidence in a wide spectrum of social institutions, including those commonly perceived to be conservative in nature.

The multifaceted character of the home education movement, however, is rarely acknowledged. Throughout this chapter, we demonstrated that despite the trends noted above the home school population is by no means monolithic. Home schools are operated by parents who are not white, not living in traditional nuclear families, and not college educated. In addition, home schools are operated not only by parents with middle-class incomes. Parent educators with limited financial resources also initiate home schools, choosing to forego additional income in order to provide their children with what they believe is the best educational opportunity. Furthermore, home schooling is not restricted to religiously oriented parents, but also includes parents whose educational choice is not to subscribe to particular religious or spiritual doctrines. Some parents, for instance, initiate home schools based on their distaste for the social and pedagogical environments that are often associated with public and private schools. These parents want to educate their children in what they believe is the best learning environment: the home. Finally, some parent educators support government funding of public education even though they do lack confidence in public schools. It is important to recognize that this support stems from the belief that public education is not inherently undesirable and a desire to maintain some contact with public schools. Parents' support for government funding is especially strong if public school services and facilities are made available to home-educating parents and their children, and we suspect that this group of parent educators

will become increasingly confident in public schools as more services and resources are offered to them and their children. We return
to this issue in Chapter 5.

In this chapter we made explicit the variety of parents who teach
their children at home and the wide range of rationales that orient
their home school activity. Merely identifying the common and
disparate characteristics of parent educators, however, both neglects
the unique experiences that shape their journey into home schooling
and glosses over their interpretations of what it means to educate
children at home. In the next chapter, we present narratives of
several parent educators to address these issues.

Notes

1. From "When Schools Fail Children" by David Guterson. Copyright © 1990 by
David Guterson. Reprinted by permission of Georges Borchardt, Inc., for the author.

2. The chi-square test of significance was used to compare characteristics of
parent educators with state and national populations. Chi-square is a nonparamet-
ric test of significance, whereby expected frequencies are compared against observed frequencies. A "significant" chi-square statistic indicates that the observed
difference between home-educating parents and either state or national populations was *not* random.

3. As some evidence suggests, the legal rights of parent educators are linked to
their ability to convince policy makers that they are educationally capable of
effectively teaching their own children. Notably, home educators maintain, on a
variety of fronts other than their educational attainment, that they are eminently
suited to teach their children at home. The most common response parent educators
make when questioned about their educational qualifications is that the intimate
knowledge and understanding they have of their children qualifies them to operate
a home school.

4

Seeing Through the Eyes of Parent Educators

Our decision [to home educate] is based on our strong feeling for parenthood and parental responsibility and our desire to allow flexibility and freedom in our child's education. Many of your [survey] questions reveal our desire to get away from school, public or private, but seem to lack the understanding that not only are we moving away but are moving to something. It's not just education, it's a way of life—a style, a family structure.

—41-year-old home school father, Washington

A s we entered the world of parent educators, we were continually struck by the manner in which they interpreted their relationship to home schooling through the lens of both past and present personal and family experiences. These moments led us to reflect upon a stereotypical image of parents who operate home schools—one of people who immediately respond to particular conventional school situations in an ill-advised and irrational manner. These images, we found, differed significantly from the interpretations and understandings parent educators attributed to their personal journey into home education.

45

Parents establish home schools for a diversity of reasons. We met parents whose religious and spiritual convictions "fit well" with the notion of teaching their children at home. Other parents told us about how the negative peer cultures associated with public schools led them to home education. Still others spoke eloquently about how their home instruction program stimulated more positive relations among family members.

Although there is diversity, we found through our intense interviews with more than 30 home-educating families several relatively consistent themes in their experiences. In this chapter, we present glimpses of these parents' experiences through the stories they tell. In the first section, we trace some of the themes that we found, highlighting the forces shaping parents' journeys into home education. In the remainder of the chapter, we present the narratives of home education parents. These narratives illustrate the complex, yet rich meanings parents associate with the activity of home schooling.

Perspectives of Parent Educators: The Central Themes

Parent educators come to the tasks and responsibilities of educating their children with a kaleidoscope of personal and family experiences. These experiences form both a backdrop and lens for their contemporary home-educating practices and perspectives. Prior family and educational experiences play a central role in the ways parents first begin to think about home education. These experiences then become primary in the development of their rationales for operating a home school (see Knowles, 1991, for an extensive discussion of these biographical/life history influences). Parent educators do not, however, engage in home school activities within a vacuum, separated from society and the communities in which they live. Their adult family and work lives also strongly influence how they perceive their particular home school and its day-to-day operation.

For the most part, parents initially consider home education in light of their interpretations of current social trends and events. The strong ties they establish with various community organizations (e.g., home school organizations, churches, parent educator support groups) provide the support usually needed to actually make the decision to begin home instruction. The organizations in which parent educators become involved reflect their particular family values and beliefs. In turn, their participation in supportive organizations plays a major role in shaping their perspectives about what it means to teach one's children at home.

Home education parents' ways of thinking about education in general and home education specifically, as well as the expectations and goals they hold for themselves and their children, are powerfully influenced by social forces and community organizations. The following discussion portrays the important role that each plays in shaping the way parent educators interpret the phenomenon of home education and come to understand their reasons for teaching their children at home.

Thinking About Home Education: Biographical Influences

As might be expected, many home school parents articulate strong views about formal education and about the educational experiences their children had or potentially could have in public and private schools. Their views about conventional schools are often integrally tied to the experiences that they had in schools while growing up. Many parent educators, therefore, tend to think about home education through the lens of their own prior experiences.

Toward one end of the spectrum are those parents who remember schools as places where they suffered psychological or physical abuse—or both—at the hands of disrespectful and mean-spirited teachers and students. Schools are also remembered as being dangerous places where personal injury and injustice were frequent and even the norm, especially for persons less able to stand up for their individual rights. These parents often feel that little has changed in conventional schools. The goal of their home school is to protect their children from incurring similar experiences.

Toward the opposite end of the spectrum are those home-educating parents who recollect pleasant, valuable, and satisfying memories of schools and classrooms, and who retell scenarios in which learning was stimulated and the relationships with teachers were warm and empowering. Although these positive schooling perspectives are less frequently articulated, many of the parents who have these fond memories simply want to replicate those satisfying kinds of experiences for their own children.

Through the lens of their experience and in light of their interpretations of current social trends and events, many parent educators come to think of themselves as more pedagogically advanced than teachers in conventional schools. Some see themselves as better able to articulate a relevant and exciting curriculum to their children, a curriculum that is not only more appropriate for their individual children's learning styles but more in tune with the pragmatic needs of the modern world. Other parent educators decry the effects of large class sizes in formal schools and believe that teachers are unable to provide individual attention to their children. As parent educators, they see themselves being more in tune with and understanding of their children's unique needs. In addition, some parents (often those who are religiously oriented) explain that teaching their children at home allows them to focus the curriculum almost exclusively on the "basics." These parents find distasteful what they perceive to be the scattered curricula and increasing humanistic and liberal expectations of conventional schools.

Making the Decision to Home Educate

Parent educators engage in a variety of exploration strategies before finally deciding to educate their children at home. Such decision making is often a prolonged affair, coming after considerable personal introspection and following many discussions about home education within and outside of the family circle. Other times it is a "snap decision," which in the case of families with children in conventional schools, appears to rest largely on some precipitous event or circumstance in the classroom or school.

The media is another important vehicle in making the decision to home school. Reading books or newspapers often alerts parents to successful home school families and the experiences that parents have educating their own children. In addition, home education advocates are increasingly visible in local communities, providing information about the potential benefits of educating children at home.

Parents who are thinking about operating a home school are often further motivated by gaining knowledge about other parents' success in teaching their own children. Prospective parent educators mine the experiences of other home-educating parents, especially those who have engaged in the practice for several years. Such experienced people are often first contacted through local or regional chapters of home school organizations and networking conferences.

Because the responsibility of educating at home is so great, parents usually make a commitment to operating a home school only after considerable thought. Being a parent educator usually entails a commitment to fairly intense work with children on a daily basis, in addition to carrying out other family and work-related responsibilities. As a result of this commitment, it is especially difficult for those parents who work outside of the home for some period of each day or week, and for single parents with meager levels of financial support. Considering that a great deal of home education is facilitated by mothers who have other home-related responsibilities, although no outside employment, their physical and psychological workloads are often extremely heavy.

Home Education and Family Life

Operating home schools can be either disruptive to or an extension of family life. In some families, the operation of a home school has a profound effect on family life, turning routines upside down. For instance, home-schooling children can become a time-consuming adjunct to a myriad of family activities, interrupting the normal daily flow of family activities, routines, and individual responsibilities. Under such circumstances, life at home is often quite stressful. This is particularly true if the activities associated with teaching and learning at home are viewed as similar to the classroom processes found in traditional schools. For other families, the impact of operating a home school is minimal because the education process is viewed holistically. Home education responsibilities merely become extensions of "normal" family activities and routines. In these families, the education process and the physical, academic, psychological, and moral development of the children have always been the center point of both family activities and parents' thinking—that is, the education of the children (defined as holistic and broad in scope) is an integral and ongoing part of family life.

Parents' Accounts:
Stories From the Home Front

What follows is a brief exploration into the experienced worlds of several parent educators. They articulate in their own voices some of the educational and family experiences that led them to home educate their children. From our many extensive parent interviews, we selected four families' narratives to present in this chapter (see Chapter 1 for a description of how these families were chosen as interview participants). We present their accounts in some depth to give a more complete picture of their perspectives and experiences. We only minimally edited their words, sometimes rearranging the texts to achieve a better flow of ideas and more accurate chronological progression of their experiences.

These accounts are not intended to be representative of the hundreds of families from whom we obtained survey data nor the many parents we interviewed. The narratives, however, do provide a sense of the parents' diversity of backgrounds, perspectives, and experiences. The narratives give a glimpse into some of the many issues and circumstances that parents face during the daily operation of a home instruction program. Their words give personal and contextual meaning to the central themes discussed above as well as to the analyses in other chapters, particularly Chapters 3 and 5. Because each parent's narrative stands alone, in a spirit of respect for the parents' perspectives, we offer no further commentary.

Roger

Roger and Danae (his wife) have been involved in home education for well over 10 years. As a leader in a state home education organization, Roger shared with Danae the responsibility of educating their two children through high school. Roger's job as a college teacher afforded him the flexibility to participate in the educational processes at home, and again with Danae, to take on prominent state leadership responsibilities. Because Danae was ill at the time of the interview, their story is told from Roger's perspective:

> I had never questioned the validity of [public] schools. [I assumed that public] school was the only way to go, and so I was not open to the idea [of home education]. At that point, [in my early years of parenting], I didn't challenge the status quo and go outside the norms of being a "normal person." I was hesitant to do that. But the more I dealt with my children in school, the more home education became something [that] I wanted.
>
> [When our son, who is now 23 years old, was in kindergarten we began to think], "We could do this better than they can! They're goofing things up right and left," but it never seriously occurred to us that we could [become home educators]. About 7 years later we heard [a prominent home educator] on television—or [maybe it was] the radio—and we said, "This is something that we ought to consider." After that we sent off for a book, and that was the turning point. From then on it was "Yeah, that's what we're going to do."
>
> [At that time our son was in grade seven in a small rural town, and in that community there] was a very narrow definition of what a young "man" is [supposed to be]. Our son didn't really fit that definition. He was his own person. He didn't hunt and he didn't want to drive a big four-wheel drive truck, so he was kind of put outside the social structure of things. He didn't fit really well and got a lot of abuse from some of the other boys and even some of the girls who felt he wasn't part of it and wasn't with them.
>
> We said to ourselves, "What do we really want our kids to be able to do? If we're going to take them out of school, what do we really want to have happen?" And then, the second question was, "How are we going to get there?" We decided that we wanted [the children] to be decision makers. We wanted them to learn how to make decisions autonomously, to gather information, to put in their value systems, and to learn how to make decisions. So everything we've done revolves around that focus. We decided in order

to get there they needed a couple of skills—the main ones were reading and math skills—and we've been pretty successful. That's kind of what's happened with our children.

[Home education] has also changed the way that we have related our religion to our children. We've come at it a lot more autonomously and we, in essence, have said, "Okay, school is a social structure that you can participate in or not participate in, and church is also. These [matters] are your decisions, and you have to make them." And we guide them through that; we hope they follow our values. I think it's put our religion in a different context for them.

We were really very excited about [the prospect of home education]. I remember telling my employer [at the time], who was also my brother-in-law, how excited I was about the possibility—and the things that were going to come out of it—and he completely negated the whole thing. He thought it was the most stupid thing that anybody could possibly do in their whole lives, that it was [going to] totally destroy my children, and [that] it was just absolutely ludicrous.

[The school] superintendent was adamantly opposed to home education, I think, primarily because it was a small district. His opposition really made us dig in our heels, solidify our ideas, and do the research we needed to do—[especially about] socialization, and how kids learn.

Most of [our friends] questioned what we were doing. Danae's folks never gave us any trouble and have always been supportive. On my side of the family, my mother (who worked in the education department of a college) never did really say anything but withdrew [from us] for a period of time—some years ago. [For a while] we hardly ever talked to each other. [But] as she's watched the children grow and dealt with them, she supports us totally. She says to us [now], "You've just got a marvelous family, they're just fantastic. They're great. You must really love 'em. They're turning out to be great people." So, I guess, the proof's in the pudding.

I had applied to be a school psychologist for the [school] district. After we started home schooling the superintendent made a statement that probably could have been used in a court of law if I had chosen to do [so]. He said. "Well you're a home schooler now, and that's [your choice]. Consideration of you being a school psychologist is out of the question now because you're a home schooler." And he was very clear about that. I said, "I'm not interested anymore in [the job]."

Our kids [are] very independent, they think for themselves, they know who they are in relation to others—their peers and other people. We have never stressed high academic achievement. We've never stressed that we did it for religious reasons. We did it for them as people, and that's the way it's turned out.

Beliefs [about education] that I hold are that children, given the right atmosphere—a combination of interest and ability to be inspired to be what they can be—will learn automatically. And they don't need to be forced, they don't need to be coerced. If it's a good thing, they'll do it, because it's a good thing to do. The role of the teacher is to set the stage so that it's interesting and useful to the student. [Children] will learn automatically. You don't have to grade, you don't have to coerce, you don't have to force, and you don't have to push. You just have to set the stage, and they'll [learn] automatically. [I know] that's kind of Pollyanna-like, but to the degree that you can put it into a system, it works. It really does!

Education, ideally, is an experience. It's an enjoyable experience, and it's a growth experience, and so it is life. It's everything that you do in and out of school. It encompasses everything, and the product of it is us, people.

I think most public educators basically think the same way I do. They hold the child as very important. They want the child to grow as an individual. But they're totally frustrated because they can't do it. I think most public educators are just frustrated people. The system won't let them [help children grow as individuals], the constraints that they have won't let them—the financial and philosophical constraints and the legislative pressures that say, "You need to be competent in this area because this is important to us, and we're going to test you here, and we're going to test you there, and we're going to demand accountability." That's really frustrating to a lot of public educators. When you get through all the flak and baloney that there is, the bottom line for a public educator and the bottom line for a home educator are the same thing.

A good home-educating parent can't just be angry at the public schools [and can't have] a negative motivation. [Their motivation] has to be positive. It has to be based on the love and desire to do the best for their children. The second thing is they need to be willing to investigate and decide for themselves. They need to be independent enough to say, "This is what I believe, and I'm going to find something out there that's going to fit me." They need to have motivation. The amount of resources they have isn't [crucial]. They could be poor or they could be rich. It's probably easier to be rich, but it isn't essential. So they need motivation and they need the ability to be independent and find a direction. They need to be able to lead themselves. Past that, they need to be smart enough to be able to figure things out, [something] the overwhelming majority of people in our society can't do. They need to be strong enough to stand up to opposition.

[More specifically home-educating parents need to] listen very carefully to their children and know where their children are mentally, socially, and emotionally. They're very close to their children so they're not a controlling, dictating type, they're a facilitator. When they see that their child needs some direction they find a way for their child to get it, rather than giving it to the child. The word "facilitator," or "guide," comes to mind. They know where they stand in relationship to their values, so they impart those values to the kids. They see that, "Okay, math is important, so we'll do some math." But they listen very carefully to what their children are saying.

[Danae] does most of the actual work with the children. She basically decides what to do, or at least up to a certain point. And she gathers the material, does the curriculum, buys the books, takes the kids to the library. We're a fairly traditional family. Danae has always wanted to stay home with the children. My role is to go out and earn the bread. She's pretty liberated, but she didn't really want to work [outside of the home]. I wanted more input with the children. I interface with the outside world lots more than Danae does—I do almost all of that. So it's kind of a natural thing for me to have input.

A lot of our spare time is [spent] with home school people and with home school activities, directing organizations and things like that. The evolution of our home school has been important to [the growth of] my educational philosophy. It has had a very direct and significant impact on the way I view my [present] job and the way I teach people how to be teachers (in my job). And it's how I make what I believe fit with the frustrations of public education. I'm very up front about it. What I tell people in my education and philosophy classes is just straight [talk]. It's not couched as home school philosophy but as *my* educational philosophy, and that's what I tell them.

Joe

With Nina, his wife, Joe has home educated their three children since they removed the eldest, now a senior in high school, from public school during his grade six year. Their commitment to home education is rooted both in their religious beliefs and in their experiences of school and family life. The excerpts that follow present Joe's perspectives on the couple's experiences as home educators and on the activity of home schooling. As in many home-educating families, Joe acted as a spokesperson for the family even though Nina is heavily involved in the education process:

I am part Blackfoot Indian. When I was younger I was as dark as the ace of spades and the abuse from others [in school] was terrible for me. My mother, a Blackfoot Indian, would tell me to beat them up. I was too demure and resented that I had to endure the humiliation of being picked on by teachers and being beat up over and over and over again. I had really bad experiences in school initially, but when Mom got wind of some of the things going on, she was dynamic [in her actions]. My woodworking teacher was the meanest cotton-pickin' man there ever was and he delighted in picking [on me] and calling me names. In tears, I would tell my mom about this guy. One day she got a baseball bat and came up [to the classroom] and called this guy out after he had paddled me. She pounded the bat on the desk and said, "If you ever touch my kid again I'm going to use this on you." Then she marched down to the principal's office, barged into a meeting, slammed the bat down on the conference table and said, "If that man ever touches my kid again, I am going to take this bat and work you both over."

I did have some good teachers. I had several who were sensitive to my inquisitive and scientific nature, and some teachers would catch fire with me and cultivate [the fire], seeing that I was interested. But there were a few [teachers] who destroyed my desire to learn.

When you grow up you think you are going to have children of your own and put them through the public school system. I mean, that is just the way it is. That's the mainstream American thing to do—send your children to a public school—but I never felt comfortable with the idea. I knew I had bad experiences with school and you do not have to read very far in the newspapers and other magazines to see clearly that the public school system is in deep trouble. So, I thought—as I started off as a young father—"I was affected by my youth and my experiences," which made it very easy to make the changes I ultimately made. Whether it was related to fear, abuse, or the teachers, I just have some very deep feelings about some of the things I have seen and experienced firsthand in the school system.

We made a commitment when we had our children that home educating is not a part-time job. It is a full-time job. We wanted to see the lights go on in our children's eyes as they learned and became educated about different things. We wanted to be there when [our eldest son] had difficult times [learning] so we could [help] him understand the [particular] concepts. A teacher in the classroom has no vested interest in going after the *Ones* [the kid who doesn't seem to understand]—and my son was one of the *Ones*. The teachers wanted to tread over the top of him—push that square kid into the round hole—and I was not going to sit still for it. So I brought him home and taught him myself, overcoming a lot of tremendous handicaps in the process. The school system was not willing to take care of his problems so I said, "He is my son. I have 100% of my time that I am willing to give to him."

We were in a real emotional upheaval and deeply resentful of the system because of what they did to my oldest son, Mike. We took him out [of school] first. The next year we took out the others. Michael was in [school until] sixth grade and we yanked him out because he was having so many problems he even began ditching school. Young people who fail are advanced through the system and their problems are not addressed. Our sixth-grade son had a third-grade ability; all of his problems were because he could not read and understand the material. He was frustrated and mad and [felt contempt toward the school] because he could not read and understand. All of my children are now avid readers. This has been one of our greatest success stories.

We are members of the Mormon Church. The world is in such a state of grave immorality, and [people] have a lack of spiritual training that has practically demoralized the whole system [and then] they took prayer and things like that out of the school system. We deeply believe that the best educational process you can be exposed to is through living God's law and learning about Him. No one could train my kids better than I can because I have a 100% interest in their education. As I have grown in my understanding of the church I have grown [in my understanding of children]. Kids need to be taught in their homes and have this indoctrination ingrained in them from the first time they are able to understand.

The school systems continue to go downhill. When we took Michael out of school, there weren't so many guns and stuff [in schools]. Just in the small amount of time we have

been involved in home schooling, the public schools have
gone from educational institutions to being a battleground.
The kids in all social strata are involved in day-to-day combat
against elements that I never had to deal with. When I was in
high school it was pretty calm—sex was hidden—and the
worst thing you could be caught doing is smoking cigarettes.

At the beginning [in our home-educating efforts] we felt
like we only had so many hours here and [needed to do] so
much cramming. You have to be cognizant of each child at
all times and it can be really stressful on you. As time went
on, we realized that getting the exemption [from attendance
in the school district] was not really the hassle it was made
out to be and we were not going to have somebody glower-
ing over our shoulders all the time. All we needed to do was
have [the children] take one test a year to make sure that [they
were making] academic progress. The pressure was taken off the
children to jump through hoops. [Our kids] were able to go at
their own speed, and when that happened, it was wonderful.

A lot of the stress came from not knowing what the school
district expected from us. They have a whole list of things
they want [home educators] to do. We worried if they were
going to check on us every 2 weeks or wanted us to save
every paper the kids did. We have packets and packets of
stuff to prove to [public school administrators] that our kids
are doing the work, but [the matter of accountability] became a nightmare for us. We had to do extra paperwork just
to show the school. The children had to take practice papers
over and over and over again, even when they knew the
material. Every year the criteria seem to change, and it
seems like the [school personnel] are trying to make it
harder and harder to get the next year's exemption.

[Teaching and learning at home] have been such a growing process for all of us. As you interact with the child you
learn about yourself and the things you may have missed
out on when you were a kid growing up. You get to live
vicariously through the eyes of your children. They can
teach each other things. It is everybody working together.
They say the teacher usually learns more. So when they help

each other, their own understanding is better. In the home school the children are always doing things together. This makes the family stronger.

We have gained a lot of confidence as time has gone on, [especially] when we see the lights go on in our kid's eyes, or when we see other young people—not only in the church but in the world—who are failing and we see that our kids are not failing. [Our kids] are succeeding. When they are tested, our kids' results are in the highest percentiles. You feel justified that you have done the right thing. We have had people tell us how intelligent and well behaved our children are, how remarkable they are. [As parents] we feel more stable, less worried [about our kids], and really good about our roles as teachers.

Training your children is a lifetime thing. You still have the responsibility—even when they are in public school—to train children in [matters of] morality and ethics, and in different things that are now not taught in the public schools. As a parent you have this responsibility to teach them about honor, and country, and things like that, things that are not being taught [in schools]. The role of teacher is a role you have from the moment you are a parent.

Toni

As a self-proclaimed feminist, Toni's commitment to home education is rooted in her long-held opposition to "mass education for children." She and her husband, both well-educated professionals, are intent on striving for independence from governmental authority and maintaining their atheistic perspectives as an appropriate milieu for educating their girls to appreciate their matriarchal heritage within a patriarchal society:

I do not put myself into situations which are harmful to me (for a variety of reasons based on the emotional and psychological abuse that [I suffered] as a child growing up). I am very sensitive to the destructiveness of those [experiences]. I will not allow my children to be forced into a situation they find threatening—emotionally or physically. It took me many years to break out of those habits, that when something felt uncomfortable you had to endure it. I was brutalized in school. I went to school in the sixties and I can remember there being a tremendous amount of drugs and violence in school. I did not want to go [to school]. There were so many stumbling blocks to even sitting in a classroom. It was overcrowded. There were not enough textbooks. There were problems of drugs and violence. I wore orthopedic shoes and the kids teased me about them. Also, I was harassed, maybe because of illness. Physically, I was just slow. My movements were slow. My mother refused to cut my hair so I had unusually long hair. And so I was taunted and teased about that.

Education on the public end has never been an option for me. I don't think it is beneficial to young children to have them get up at a certain time and go through this ritual of getting dressed and eating at a time when they may not be particularly hungry (at 6 or 7 in the morning). The government tells little kids, "You will get up at this time, you will eat at this time, you will play at this time, you will be at this building at this time, you are going to study this course at this time for this many minutes, and you are going to go whether you want to or not. This is what you will do." I think it is dehumanizing, exploitive. I think it is damaging.

I was about 17 when I came to the conclusion that I had to take responsibility for my own education. You don't assume responsibility in just one area without it impacting all the other areas in your life. I had my children at home because hospitals are institutions where people have bankrolls, people go to work at specific times, doctors come in at specific times—everything is run on a schedule. I took responsibility for the birthing of my children. It never occurred to me that I would relinquish responsibility for educating them.

I [home] birthed our children. This was very political. Nursing them was very political. Educating my children is very political and very lonely. I did not realize when I was alone and wore the cloak of anonymity in this society that nobody cared that I was just a little off center and not marching to the same drummer that everybody else marched to. But the moment I had children, I had this cloak of anonymity ripped off of me and I came under some harsh and unusual criticism.

I fundamentally do not believe in mass education for children. I am a self-defined feminist. I have a different educational program. I have females. I want them to be aware of their history and their ancestors' contributions to who they are today. I grew up in a patriarchal society and in an educational system which is patriarchal. I was not engaged when I was a senior in high school. I was not married when I was 21. My father said to me that I was disgracing the family because I did not even have a prospect of a husband. I was supposed to be married, barefoot, and pregnant, but that was just not my calling.

It took me a long time to find out who I was, and what I came from, and this was stuff I had to learn on my own. In the government of even a private educational system, the curriculum is going to be slanted toward men. Obviously, they have made significant contributions to society as well; however, my species has made equal contributions and this is something I want my children to find out when they are young, not when they reach the age of maturity and are sup-posed to interact with their government and they are wonder-ing, "Who am I?" I want them—at an impressionable age—to have the beginnings of a solid and firm foundation from which to operate when they are ready to go out on their own.

Home education is a misnomer [and there are stereotypes associated with the term]. I do not sit around the dining room table wearing a calico dress instructing my children on the Holy Bible. Unfortunately, [those with] hostile opin-ions are trying to portray home educators as some sort of freaks, or people trying to keep themselves rooted in the past, that somehow are not futuristic thinking, and they do not want to evolve. I think I am the only home educator in this state who is an atheist, which sets me apart from other home educators. I think home education more appropri-ately should be defined as parental control education. I indoctrinate my children and I do so unapologetically. I brainwash them, if you will. I pass on my intellectual DNA, impact their environment, impact their psyche and the way their brain grows and matures. I think that is the essence of how children make us immortal. That is how we directly impact our children. Today, children are being impacted by a machine—government. When you think of children—how much is going on physiologically in their bodies—and [ask] "What is the major influence?" the [answer] is not "The family." It is that machine out there. That is what is manipulating them.

I consider myself a child expert, an education expert. Talking about [education] and experimenting with it and knowing [that] some things work and some things do not. I do not like busywork. I do not like memorizing things for no reason. There are some things which need to be memorized because it makes other things easier. A case in point was when my daughter was moving into algebra and had to memorize the multiplication tables. That was one of the rare times I said to her that she had to memorize them because by not being good [at them] would create large obstacles.

My husband is a brilliant man. He knows a lot about a lot of things. His influence on the children is one where he demands high intellectual standards. You cannot be lazy around him because he will chew you up and spit you out. He is real challenging and consequently the children have a kind of odd sense of humor bordering on the bizarre. My kids have adult friends because, as a parent, I cannot pretend that I can meet the needs of my kids all the time. So it is nice that they have that interaction. We have in our lives adults who are caring and nurturing. They have something to offer intellectually and are willing to share this with our children.

Loricia

A single mother, Loricia describes herself as "handicapped due to a physical deformity of [her] feet." A bachelor of science degree with a major in child development enabled Loricia to support herself and her son financially, first as a teacher in the private school her son attended for 3 years and later as a home educator of her own and other children. Loricia's son is now a community college student preparing to transfer to a university:

> [Initially], I sent [my son] to an excellent kindergarten. He was in a reasonably small class—18 kids—with a teacher with 16 years of experience. It was a good, warm, nurturing atmosphere. I had no complaint about it, but I very carefully watched his papers coming home and they were ludicrous! [He was doing] things he could have done when he was 3 years old. I had taught him certain things because I wanted to make up for problems in the system. For example, relatives told me that teachers didn't have enough time to teach a child to write decently, so I thought, "Well, that's fine. I can [teach him]. I know how to write. I'll teach him manuscript printing." And so I taught him a good deal before he ever went to school. His skill wasn't sharp but it was basically laid down. [In kindergarten] they didn't attempt to write anything; it was just little picture work.
>
> [At a parent night] I visited the teacher to let her know that my child was capable of a lot more than what was offered. Somehow or other I got the message, "Look, I know your kid can do more than we're doing, but this is where we're at. Don't expect us to do anything else." I was horrified! There were other things, like virtual fist fights on the kindergarten playground [that were not being resolved], and some things going on in the bathroom. [For example,] my son said, "Because the latch on the door didn't work, the kids would come in and look at you, or pinch you." I thought, "This is silly!" I started asking friends questions about other [educational] options and ultimately I visited a private school. Fortunately, they were willing to take him. I gave them a very small amount of money [because] I was poor and penniless. I repaired their books and worked in their library to defray the expenses of his tuition. The next year, they invited me to teach there.
>
> After spending 3 years with the private school I became aware of some administrative problems with the school. I also had this constant problem: I was a single parent and

had to make an income, yet I needed to raise my son, and not just have him be a latchkey child! At that point I said, "Okay, if there is anyway that I can conduct a private school out of my own home, I'm going to do that." So that's what we did. I ran a small private school—kindergarten and first grade—and eventually I took on some second and third graders. We ran home school very differently than most people. I worked with my son [very early] in the morning and [very late] at night [because] during the days (when it was his study time) I worked with the other kids.

Generally speaking, we would be up about 5:30 in the morning, when we had time for planning and scripture reading. At that point in time, if I was "with it," I made a list of basic assignments for him to do during the day. It was standard [procedure] that if he finished everything on the list he got free reading time. By the time he was 7 or 8 years old he was "free reading" stuff by Mark Twain like Huck Finn. In my view, one of the greatest advantages of home schooling is the opportunity to free read—where someone is not going to test you about what you read, or make you necessarily write papers on what you read. You simply get to read. And in our case, a lot of times, we just talked about [what we had read] because it was fun!

School usually started about 8 or 8:30 for my regular students, which meant that [my son] started studying then. My school would go [anywhere] from 1:30 in the afternoon to 2:30 or 3. About 3 o'clock, there were things like music lessons or scouting activities. If there weren't those kind of things, I would try to grab his work immediately and correct it to find out where we were at for the next day. And then, of course, there were meals and evening activities, and so on. Sometimes it was 10 o'clock at night when we were correcting things.

[In deciding to operate a home school] I was not trying to make a statement about public schools, although I am totally convinced that public schools are not dependable anymore. You cannot depend on a public school system to deliver what you intended them to deliver. You might get in a special situation where you in fact do have a good experience. But you can't depend on it anymore. I was simply determined that if there was any way, as a single parent, of raising my child, and having him decently educated, and decently brought up with a reasonable kind of Christian character, [home education] was what I was going to do.

I saw an opportunity with home schooling for kids to be able to read freely, and discuss freely, views of all kinds, including religious views. I saw opportunities that could not be got in the public schools, not only because of the curriculum, but simply by virtue of time. One of the blessings of home schooling is that you've got time—even in our situation where I was also trying to run a business. It was no easy thing. If you asked me if it was all positive and glorious and wonderful, "Heavens, no!" It was very difficult. There were [many difficult] moments because [my son] was normal and bright, and difficult to deal with at times. But I saw [home school] as an opportunity to discuss many things about my own religious background. At the age of 12 and 13 he ate [these discussions] up like you wouldn't believe—and would dive in for more.

My view is that school should basically be a place where children learn skills. As far as values go, decent Christian conduct should be upheld. In any school system chaos should never be allowed to exist. I am not talking about supertight, confined situations, but the idea that it's okay to have a classroom where children are not disciplined, where they are not learning, where they are not put in a situation where they're either expected to learn or in some cases almost allowed to learn, to me is a disaster. It does not prepare them for a life, where they're going to be expected to be able to have self-control and discipline and skills. A school system ought to have systems put together in such a way that children cannot fail.

My basic reason for taking my son out of school was not because I really had anything immense against the public system, except that it is failing. It was obvious that there were people who were more than willing to allow my child

to fail in it. And I was not going to let that happen. In a lot
of ways, public schools dampen a desire to learn. Sometimes they will not let a child broaden out and explore areas
that really interest them, sometimes they constrict. At the
same time, they sometimes don't make kids work hard
enough to [acquire] skills. Its very hard for me to see children fail. It's very hard for me to see children growing up
who are not having experiences that will allow them to
mature and grow well. For my own son, I want the doors
open at the end of high school. An 18-year-old ought to have
a wide range of options and not be so narrowed by their
own inabilities so that they can't go through the doors that
they'd like to. I couldn't have that happen to my child—or
any child that came within my influence.

I should probably say that I was not the kind of home
schooler who began with the feeling that I had no background—or that I had no capability of doing it—mainly
because I had taught a couple of years before I ever began
to home school. Even so, I had problems to solve and
massive decisions to make. [Of] most [concern] were problems of how in the world to balance a single parent existence: trying to earn an income, dealing with my child, home
schooling, and working in the church. The balance of time
constraints was a constant difficulty—it still is. The constant
strain of doing all the stuff for him, all the stuff for the home,
keeping the financial world together, playing both Mom
and Mr. Mom. The agony was trying to keep everything
going.

I did discover that in some cases home schooling took a
lot more struggling with personal and personality issues
because I had to be a parent to my child as well as a teacher.
And so, you were the big ogre sometimes, and the big bad
mom. Because there was no father in the home it made
[home educating] even more difficult. There were times that
were far more negative than [those that I experienced] as a
professional teacher, and I didn't anticipate that at the start.
There were [times when] I would threaten to send him to
public school. I've heard other home-schooling parents say

pretty much the same thing, "If you're not gonna learn from me, you're gonna learn from somebody! So you're gonna go to school if you're not gonna do work for me!" And so I thought it was tougher to be a home-schooling teacher and parent than it was to just be a professional teacher.

In many ways, home schooling and the whole experience of single parenting, because they all came together for me at the same time, forced me to evaluate and prioritize so many things [in order to] figure out what was most important, what could be let go, and what was critical to hang on to. In that way, I'm very grateful to have had the experience. I can honestly say I've experienced some things I'd rather not have to go through twice. I did not like single parenting! I do not believe in raising kids that way. I do not ever want to do that again like that. I'd raise more kids, but I want a two-parent family.

My one advice to single parents is whether you do home school or whether you do public school, be home! Somehow! That doesn't mean you have to keep your head there every minute of the day, but connect with your kids, know what's going on in their lives and engineer things on their behalf.

5

The Relationship Between Home Schools and Conventional Schools

PARENTS' PERSPECTIVES

We would like to see the day when home school parents and public school teachers could come together, share, and glean information from each other in order to assist each other. Sometimes I have questions about problems I encounter when teaching some subjects and need input. I could also use suggestions on various methods to present subjects, especially math. We need to support each other, where and when we can.

—31-year-old home school mother, Utah

Please, please, just leave us alone. I don't want anything from the school district except for them to leave my family alone and let us handle our children as we see fit.

—35-year-old home school father, Nevada

In Chapters 3 and 4, we suggested that the decision made by parents to educate their children at home extends beyond the particular educational disagreements they have with conventional schools. It included their perceptions about what constitutes the proper relationship between families, the education of children, and conventional schools. We found that the sentiment of the home school community toward conventional schools is disparate and conflicting, as illustrated earlier by the quotations from parent educators. Some parents seek assistance from conventional schools, whereas others clearly reject any attempts to cooperate or collaborate with the schools in their communities. In this chapter, we expand our analysis by examining the tenuous and often abrasive relationships that exist between home-educating parents and professional education communities. In the first two sections of this chapter, we describe and discuss the types of assistance, resources, and services that parents either desire or reject as they educate their children at home. In the third section, we briefly review the literature on cooperation between home schools and conventional schools and describe some cooperative programs established in recent years.

What Do Parent Educators Want?
What Do They Reject?

Availability and Use of Resources and Services

Our mail survey asked home-educating parents what resources and services public schools are made available to them and which ones they use in their home instructional programs. Table 5.1 shows that a relatively large percentage of parents do not know whether the public schools in their communities make any services or resources available to home education families. When resources are available and known about, however, few parents use them. The public school services and resources most likely to be used are achievement testing (14%), certain classes (14%), school textbooks (13%), and school libraries (11%). Home-educating families use special

TABLE 5.1 Availability and Use of Public School Resources by Home Educators (in percentages)

Service/Facility	Available and Used	Available Not Used	Not Available	Don't Know if Available
Achievement testing	14	44	6	37
Certain classes	14	47	10	30
Public school textbooks	13	30	14	43
Public school libraries	11	32	10	43
School sports programs	8	38	14	41
Field trips	5	16	16	63
Health screening	4	19	12	65
Club membership	4	20	11	65
Special education classes	3	28	10	59
Counseling	3	20	11	65
Psychological services	1	18	10	70

NOTE: Totals may not equal 100 due to rounding.

education classes (3%), counseling (3%), and psychological services (1%) the least.

The comments parents wrote on the survey suggest several reasons for these outcomes. Some parents simply have no interest in receiving any help from educators or educational institutions, even when they know that public school services and resources are available to home school families. Other parents are uninformed about the availability of services and resources because they have no interest in associating with public schools. As one father succinctly stated: "I don't want any services from public schools because I do not want any obligation to the public school system." Other parents indicated, however, that they are willing to use the resources and services provided by public schools, but they are not knowledgeable about what is available to them and their children. These parents typically blame their lack of knowledge on the fact that they rarely exchange information with professional educators:

> I need a list of what is available from my local school, such as dates of assemblies, field trips, topical studies, etcetera,

before the school year begins. [This would] enable us to use what we choose.

It is my understanding that the services [listed on the survey] should be made available to my children. Although we asked [the school administrator], we have not been notified of what is available.

Views on Educational and Social Services

The survey also asked home-educating parents a more general question: "What type of educational resources do you need or want to be made available to your home instruction program?" Table 5.2 demonstrates that a large percentage of parent educators wish to enroll their children part-time in extracurricular activities (81%) and academic courses (76%), and they also desire to make use of public school libraries and curricular materials (64%). This desire does not mean, however, that these parents would actually use the resources if they are available (see Table 5.1).

Several other findings make this result more understandable. For example, Table 5.2 demonstrates that parent educators have the least interest in receiving help and resources from certified teachers who *are* connected to the school district (38%). However, when parents are asked if they would accept help and resources from certified teachers *not* connected to the school district, almost one half (49%) indicated they would. Similarly, over one half of the parents (60%) expressed an interest in receiving guidance on effective teaching methods for the home education setting (the reference to "certified teachers" and "school districts" was eliminated from this survey question). Clearly, parent educators are more likely to accept educational resources and assistance when it is not governed or regulated by government school district personnel.

Table 5.2 also shows that approximately one third of the parents that we surveyed are undecided about receiving help and resources from certified teachers, whether or not the teacher is affiliated with a school district. We suspect that this indecisiveness stems from their inclination to protect the educational autonomy that is associated with home-based instruction. One mother we surveyed illustrated this point by describing her ambivalence over incorporating the resources of conventional schools into her child's instructional program:

> The more available resources are, the better. But only if the availability of materials, resources, and teachers does not imply restrictions as well. I have been advised not to use the school's [resources], unless I don't mind strings attached.

The survey also asked parents about the social resources they feel are important to the operation of a home school. The majority (86%) indicated that home school support groups and organizations are an essential part of the home education experience (see Table 5.2). This outcome is not surprising considering the studies that found home school organizations are the primary arena where parents gather resources for their instructional programs, and more important, receive the moral support they need to continue educating their children at home (Bishop, 1991; Hadeed, 1991; also see Chapter 2). The written comments of one mother describe the possible services that support groups could offer home-educating families:

> It is nice to have home school organizations with home schoolers assisting each other and sharing their individual talents. Groups could form like co-ops to cut down on the cost of supplies. A library could be organized providing homeschoolers with books, reference materials, equipment, National Geographic videotapes, along with other educational materials an individual may not be able to afford.

Parent educators also mentioned other types of social resources that are important as they educate their children at home. For instance, the majority (92%) found that the support and encouragement that they receive from families, friends, churches, and their community is integral to the process of home schooling. In addition, many parents (72%) seek accessible research on home education. During the interviews, these parents seemed eager to hear about the results of our research and many of them requested information about other home school studies that had been conducted. Although

TABLE 5.2 Educational and Social Resources Home Educators Desire (in percentages)

Support Services	Feel They Need or Want	Do Not Need or Want	Undecided
Enroll child in extracurricular events	81	9	10
Enroll child part-time in academic courses in public or private school	76	10	14
Use of public school libraries/materials	64	17	19
Help and resources from certified teacher not connected to school district	49	21	30
Help and resources from school district certified teacher	33	38	29
Guidance on effective teaching methods for home education	60	21	18
Support/encouragement from family, friends, church, and community	92	4	4
Home school support group to continue functioning or one to begin	86	5	9
More organized and effective state home school organization or one established	61	20	19
More accessible research on home schools	72	9	19

NOTE: Totals may not equal 100 due to rounding. Responses were to a 5-point Likert scale. Percentages given combine "strongly agree and agree" and "strongly disagree and disagree."

most of these parents expressed a willingness to read research reports that might challenge them to rethink or change their educational practices, they typically explained their interest in the research by describing why the findings are valuable to the home education community:

> We need more research done [on home schools] and published in order to educate the general public about the successful children who are educated in home schools.

Views on Financial Resources

Educational voucher and tax credit systems that allow parents to choose schools for their children is a topic that is widely debated across the nation (Astin, 1992; Coleman, 1992). Little discussion has occurred, however, regarding whether or not home-educating parents should be allowed to use the voucher or tax credit as a financial resource for their home instruction program. In the near future, it is likely that some form of an educational tax credit or tuition voucher will be implemented in a number of states. Therefore the survey asked home-educating parents to express their views on this issue.

Table 5.3 shows that many parents favor the idea of receiving financial assistance for the education of their children, if the assistance can be used to help finance home instruction programs. Parent educators are more likely to favor financial assistance provided by state or federal governments; they are less likely to favor assistance provided by an agency other than the government. Many of the parents' written comments speak to this issue. Some parents favor the prospect of government-funded financial aid, whereas others readily eschew monetary assistance from the government and are more inclined to seek support for their home-schooling activities from other sources:

> Any [tax] laws that support the family, should, in turn, support home schoolers. For example, mothers are given a tax credit for paying baby-sitters, so why should I be penalized for taking care of our children?

Instead of looking to the government for financial support, I would like to see a strong local support group organized that would provide educational classes for me. I would like the group to present classes on a regional or county basis, with mail-outs sent to parents describing the class, location, cost, etcetera. This type of organization is necessary for home schools, but would require time and money, and that is where the hitch comes in. Who pays for it?

Table 5.3 also shows that a smaller, yet notable percentage (13%-15%) of parent educators lack interest in obtaining financial support for home education, regardless of the funding source. Furthermore, a notable percentage (14%-33%) remain undecided about support-ing financial assistance for home schools. The numerous written comments to this question clearly suggest that these responses are related to the question of who would ultimately control home education programs. The following kinds of rationales are typically given for the views parents express about this issue:

It depends on how much say the government will have. Help and cooperation is great, but only if it allows the home school to function in its beliefs and purposes.

Tuition assistance would help, but then the government would try to tell us how, when, and what we could teach; that would defeat the purpose of home education.

We don't really need help, but it would be nice to have a "rent-a-teacher-pool." If you found yourself tearing your hair out over spelling or math, it would be neat to be able to pick up the phone and hire someone for only that subject for a while, not forever. If my plumbing leaks, I want the plumber to stop the leak, and I'm happy to pay for the work. I don't want [the plumber] to move in and insist on install-ing thermal windows and remodeling the kitchen.

Finally, the majority (61%) of parents believe that they should be exempt from paying taxes that support public school programs and do

TABLE 5.3 Home Educators' Views on Financial Assistance (in percentages)

Type of Assistance	Would Like	Would Not Like	Undecided
State or federal government tax credits or tuition vouchers for home education	71	15	14
Tax credits or tuition vouchers for home education from source other than federal government	54	13	33
To be free from taxation that supports public schools only	61	20	19

NOTE: Totals may not equal 100 due to rounding. Responses were to a 5-point Likert scale. Percentages given combine "strongly agree and agree" and "strongly disagree and disagree."

not help to support home education programs. This outcome is not surprising in light of parent educators' intense commitment to teaching their children at home (see Chapter 3). As is clearly seen in the following written responses, some parents are quite adamant about this issue:

> Our taxes pay for school materials and I think we [parent educators] should either get funds [for home education materials] or not have to pay taxes. I would like funds to purchase textbooks. And, since tax dollars purchase textbooks for children to use in public schools, that is what I seek also.

> I desire to not pay taxes. We home school and must buy our own educational materials. But we still pay taxes on two pieces of land to support two local [public] school districts.

A much smaller percentage of parents are either willing to pay taxes for public education (20%) or undecided about the tax issue

(19%). Apparently one segment of the home school population is likely to affiliate with the local schools in their communities at some point in time. This survey result probably is predictable, because home schools are occasionally established as a stopgap, providing parents with the short-term opportunity to offer their children specialized or remedial instruction. We can speculate that these parents are less hesitant than other parents to favor taxes for public education. One mother's written comments proposed a tax solution that acknowledges both the families who home school without any involvement with public schools and those who home school while also utilizing the services of public schools:

> The best system, it seems to me, would be to give parents options—how much tax paid in relationship to how much involvement they want with public schools. To educate children as we see fit is our right as parents and we are willing to pay for this right in an appropriate manner.

What Have We Learned?

In Chapters 3 and 4, we saw that home-educating parents, although coming from diverse backgrounds, are uniformly protective of their individual right to operate a home school. It should come as no surprise, then, that their perceptions of a satisfactory relationship between home schools and conventional schools are characterized by a desire to protect the autonomy and independence of their home education program. For some parents, this protection means avoiding contact with conventional schools altogether. For others, however, the exemplary relationship is one where parents and their children use the resources and services provided by conventional schools at their own discretion, that is, flexibly and without regulation.

These perceptions also influence parent educators' decisions about the particular resources and services they make use of while educating their children at home. Many parents wish to augment their instructional programs with educational resources and services, but only those that do not conflict with either the ideological or pedagogical beliefs on which their home school program is built. Many also are unwilling to accept services and resources that are not designed for the explicit purpose of assisting home-educating families. Thus organizations that directly service home schools, such as local home education support groups and statewide home school organizations, receive strong support from parent educators. As a result, parent educators generally believe that the most beneficial resources come from sources outside of conventional schools— sources that are least likely to impinge on the independence and autonomy of their home school programs.

There are some additional data in our findings to suggest that foremost in the minds of many parent educators is the task of finding ways to gather additional resources for their instructional programs while preserving the autonomy of their home school. For instance, some parents reason that the public school services and resources paid for by their tax dollars should be available if and when they choose to use them. Many parents also believe that the federal government should provide home-educating families with financial assistance in the form of a tax credit or tuition voucher, which could then be used to purchase educational resources and materials of their choosing. For similar reasons, parent educators generally are in favor of being exempt from paying taxes that support public schools and offer no financial assistance to home schools.

Finally, our findings suggest that many parent educators are eager for more studies on home education to be conducted. Much of the available research has already proved valuable in their pursuit of assistance from others who are not familiar with the potential benefits and successes associated with home education. Additional research, they reason, would further the goal of legitimating home schooling as an acceptable educational alternative, thereby facilitating the enactment of policies that allow home schools to retain their distinctive features.

These findings raise the question: To what extent can or should relations be established between conventional schools and home schools? It is clear that the ideological and pedagogical convictions that brought some parents to home education makes their participation in cooperative ventures with conventional schools unlikely (see Chapter 3 for more discussion of these convictions). A core of parent educators clearly reject any service or assistance that conventional schools might offer to home-educating families. Their explicit intention is to operate a fully autonomous and independent home school.

Although the question of cooperation is unimaginable to some home-educating parents, attempts at developing cooperative programs should not be paralyzed. Other parents clearly wish to utilize the resources and services of conventional schools. The participation of these parents, however, is equally clearly related to the degree to which their involvement with conventional schools would limit or restrict the home instructional programs that they choose to design. These parents need to know not only what services conventional schools offer to home school families, but most important, what their participation and cooperation would entail.

The relationships that exist between home-educating families and conventional schools, therefore, are tenuous. Successful relationships are dependent upon both home-educating parents' and professional educators' perceptions about the nature of cooperation between home schools and conventional schools. These perceptions derive less from idiosyncratic behaviors than from differing conceptualizations and definitions of autonomy and choice. For example, cooperative programs can be interpreted to mean that conventional schools will allow home-educating families to use school resources and services, and consequently administrators will regulate home instructional programs. On the other hand, cooperative programs could mean that home-educating families who choose to interact with conventional schools would be provided with the resources without regulations or restrictions attached.

From the perspectives of the home-educating parents we studied, the latter definition of cooperation is the one most likely to facilitate the development of productive relationships. Ray (1992b) suggests the spirit for pursuing productive cooperation:

> Home educators are exploring the difference between cooperation with conventional school educators and government officials and co-optation by them. Home educators want to be sure that there is a respectful and candid exchange

of ideas and resources. They want to be sure that, when they interact with conventional educators, they are not being taken over through assimilation into an established group or culture. (p. 29)

The Slow Movement Toward Cooperation

Cooperation between home educators and conventional schools is not a new idea. It is based on the assumption that involving home-educating parents and their children in conventional school programs will enhance both the performance of home-educated children and the academic and social environment of conventional schools. In the early 1980s, for instance, John Holt wrote about how conventional schools could benefit from working with home school families and accepting home-educated children into their programs. He argued that home-educated children could bring to local schools "considerable energy, enthusiasm, intelligence, self-motivation, [and] independence" (Holt, 1983, p. 394).

Some years later, several home education researchers expanded on Holt's thoughts and proposed several ways in which communities, conventional schools, and home education families could serve each other advantageously. Knowles (1989) suggested that local schools could encourage home education parents to participate on advisory committees and parent teacher associations. Local schools could welcome home-educated students into experiential learning activities (e.g., art and music) and large group or team activities (e.g., band and athletics). In return, school districts could receive funding in proportion to the involvement of home-educated children in their programs.

Mayberry (1992) suggested that centers for continuing higher education could draw from a range of community resources and provide home education parents with courses, information, and training. The variety of community members (including public school personnel and home school researchers) brought together in these programs could create an arena within which contrasting perspectives on home education could be discussed and worked through. In turn, positive relations among communities, schools, and home-educating parents could be enhanced. These interactions could be advantageous to conventional schools and the children that they teach by promoting what James Coleman (1988) calls "social capital," or strong and cohesive relations among family members and others in the community. Previous research has demonstrated that social capital positively influences educational achievement and attainment (Coleman & Hoffer, 1987; Kachel, 1989).

In line with these suggestions, some professional educators have gone beyond simply acknowledging that they may have home-educated students in their schools. For instance, the Holt Associates' publication, *Growing Without Schooling* (*GWS*), provides to its members a list of school districts that volunteer to be listed in *GWS* as "willingly and happily cooperating with home educators" (*Growing Without Schooling*, 1994, p. 37). Among other things, the school districts that are listed in *GWS* provide policy and legal information to families and allow parent educators and their children access to school facilities and activities such as music classes and intramural athletic programs. Numerous private schools are also actively encouraging the part-time enrollment of home-educated children. By admitting part-time students and charging prorated tuition, these schools offer a service or activity that some parent educators and their children desire.

In addition, public school laws in some states (e.g., Maine, Oregon, and Washington) now require that home-educated children be allowed to participate in interscholastic activities. In other states, boards of education have initiated or are proposing more encompassing educational programs for home school children. For example, in California, some county departments of public education instituted independent study programs (ISP) that enroll home-educated children in public schools. The home education families receive services such as consulting assistance from state-employed teachers, newsletters, ideas for field trips, and some instructional materials. In turn, public schools receive "average daily attendance" money for each student.

These examples illustrate the growing number of cooperative programs nationwide. It appears that many professional educators are now taking home schools seriously. Thus it is likely that home-educating parents are increasingly receptive to the idea of participating in cooperative ventures, even when such ventures are sponsored by public education administrations. This participation seems highest in cooperative programs that preserve the independence of home schools by allowing parent educators discretion in the use of the resources and services conventional schools provide.

In Chapter 2 we briefly discussed one model of cooperation. This model grew out of year-long negotiations between parent educators and school district officials in San Diego, California, who were interested in establishing a cooperative program. The negotiations resulted in the development of the Community Home Education program (CHE). The CHE program is explicitly designed to benefit both home-educating parents and public schools. It provides parent educators with tax-supported services and resources, and the public schools receive extra funding per student and the commitment of the home education parents who use public services. The program also is designed to maximize the services and resources available to parent educators but minimize the school district's control over home schools. A brief description of the CHE program illustrates these points:

The San Diego School District notifies parents who are considering home educating their children about the CHE program and advises them of the district's expectations for parents who enroll. Once in the program, the district provides parents with a complete set of textbooks for each child, as well as in-service activities and curriculum guides for their own use. These materials are to be used as the home school's core curriculum, but parents may supplement them with any other materials they wish. Parents are asked to prepare weekly lesson plans and submit copies to the program coordinator each month, along with samples of their children's work. In addition, the CHE program offers weekly hands-on science experiences for home-educated students; operates a computer laboratory staffed with a full-time teacher and teacher's aide; organizes frequent field trips for home-educating families; conducts networking meetings for parents, providing them the opportunity to meet and discuss their home school experiences with others; meets with individual parents three times a year to evaluate the progress of the home school program; sends out a bimonthly newsletter with information about services, activities, and community events; and provides books and audiovisual materials to parent educators. CHE now accommodates over 180 students, employs six full-time teachers, and provides a full range of services to home school families (Dalaimo, in press; San Diego County Office of Education, 1988, 1990).

What do these models tell us? First, they remind us of the often-overlooked fact that parent educators and educational professionals do successfully cooperate. Second, such cooperation clearly can occur in numerous ways. Third, the success of cooperative programs is dependent largely upon finding a balance between the individualistic stance of many home-educating parents and the state's interest in educational matters. Primary to both groups are the educational conditions that result from effective cooperative ventures.

We would be foolish to ignore, however, the various perspectives and points of view regarding the relationship between families and public education that mark the tenuous relationship between home-educating parents and the educational establishment. To assume that cooperative programs will be embraced immediately by either parent educators or educational professionals would be unwise. Cooperation is unquestionably a subject needing further inquiry.

6

Implementation of Policies and Views of Superintendents

Home schooling should not be the responsibility of the state.

—Public school superintendent, Utah

School districts should try to help [home education families] give the best possible instruction to their children.

—Public school superintendent, Washington

School superintendents should probably look very closely at the reasons why parents are turning away from public schools and teaching their children at home.

—Public school superintendent, Nevada

In the previous three chapters, we explored home education from the vantage point of the parents who teach their children. In this chapter, we shift our focus to the perspectives of school superintendents who implement the state statutes and school district policies that govern home schools. We begin by briefly summarizing the home education statutes and policies in Washington, Utah, and Nevada. We then examine the survey responses of the school superintendents in these states to illustrate their perceptions and interpretations of the policies that govern home schools and the parents who operate them. Although school superintendents' understandings of home education policies and home-educating parents may seem unconnected to the discussion in previous chapters, our findings suggest relationships in how policies are implemented. Consequently, the manner in which superintendents implement home school policy affects the daily operation of home schools. In the final section of the chapter, we briefly discuss the policy implications of our analysis.

The findings discussed in this chapter were drawn from the survey responses of 118 school district superintendents in Washington, Nevada, and Utah (see Chapter 1 for a detailed discussion of the superintendent survey). In each state, the implementation of state policies regarding home education falls under the domain of the school district superintendents. Although our findings are limited to an analysis of superintendents in these three western states, we believe that the policy issues raised in this chapter should be considered by professional educators and policy makers throughout the country.[1]

Home Education Laws and Policies

Home education is usually addressed in state legislation in one of three ways. Most frequently, home education is permitted as an exemption to the state's compulsory school attendance act. A second, and also quite common occurrence, is for states to include home schools in the private school statute, regulating them in much the same way as other private schools in the state. A third form of legislation that is appearing with greater frequency, especially in states where home education has been formally recognized or legalized within the past decade, is a specific statute dealing with the establishment and operation of home schools. Nevada and Utah, two of the earliest states in the nation to legalize the practice of home education, fit into the first category, permitting home schooling as an exemption to the compulsory attendance law. Washington, which more recently legalized home education, falls into the third category and has specific statutes addressing home education.

In part, the respective states' home education laws are products of history, reflecting public beliefs and attitudes about home education at the time the laws were written. In Utah, for example, where laws regulating home schools were enacted in 1953, no provisions were made to permit home-educated children access to public school services or facilities, including interscholastic athletic participation. The Nevada administrative regulations, enacted in 1956, allowed local school district officials to decide whether home-educating parents and their children may use public school services and facilities. Both states' laws mirror the conventional wisdom of the era in which they were enacted, an era when the home school was not generally considered a legitimate educational setting (see Chapter 2). In Washington, however, the home school law enacted in 1985 gave home-educating families broad access to public school services and facilities, including interscholastic athletic programs. Thus the current trend toward greater cooperation between home schools and public schools, as described in Chapter 5, is evident in more recently enacted legislation.

Local school district policies regarding home education in Nevada, Utah, and Washington vary in focus, scope, and detail. They share a common bond in the extent to which they replicate their respective states' home education laws. In Washington, for example, the home education statute is lengthy, addressing issues ranging from parental qualifications necessary to home educate through home-educating parents' rights of access to public schools, and the local school district policies are similarly inclusive and detailed. In Utah, on the other hand, the law is considerably more vague, and local school district policies are generally brief, speaking only to the particular points mentioned in the law and leaving many decisions about specific details (e.g., parental qualifications to home educate and the appropriateness of the home school curriculum) to the discretion of individual school district superintendents. Nevada is the only state among the three in which the state board of education established a set of administrative regulations outlining substantive issues related to the home education law. Thus, although the Nevada law itself is very general, the regulations make implementation similar to that in Washington in that both states offer clear guidelines for superintendents to use in making decisions about home education.

In all three states, then, the local school district home education policies resemble the state law, structurally and substantively. Furthermore, many school districts' policy statements include verbatim sections from the state home education statutes. The laws in the three states, however, differ with respect to (a) procedures for granting parents exemptions from the state compulsory attendance law to home educate; (b) compliance obligations of parent educators (including curriculum requirements, record keeping, assessment of home-educated children); (c) policies governing the reentry of students into public schools; and (d) special education services offered to home-educated children (see Marlow, 1992, for a detailed discussion of how these laws differ in each state).

Although the home education statutes differ in several ways regarding the scope of the compliance requirements, as well as the level of access for families to public schools, none of the laws appear to be constructed as barriers to home education. Their primary regulatory aspects focus on student achievement and outcomes, with annual testing or reviews of student performance as a consistent requirement. Parental requirements regarding teaching qualifications and home school instructional practices are rarely addressed in mandates. None of the states require parents to possess college degrees or teaching certificates to home educate their children, nor do they require the use of specific curricular materials. Furthermore, where exemptions to home educate must be renewed, renewal is done on an annual basis, and parent educators are not required to be subjected to frequent or periodic compliance reviews or monitoring. The local policies in all states typically devolve authority for oversight of compliance issues, such as assessing parental qualifications or determining the educational equivalence of home school curriculum and instruction, to school principals, with district superintendents retaining final decision-making authority. Thus local school district policies do not advocate or promote home education, but they tend to minimize regulation and facilitate compliance.

Within these legal frameworks, school superintendents must implement local policies regarding home schools, and the final decision-making authority rests on their shoulders. Therefore it is important to understand how superintendents learn about the legal statutes, and more important, learn about parent educators and their home schools.

Superintendents' Knowledge and Perceptions

Superintendents in Washington, Utah, and Nevada possess discretionary authority to make decisions that affect home-educating parents. In many instances, the scope of their authority in policy matters is considerable. The first task in policy implementation is for key players to understand the basic compliance factors underlying particular policies—to know the rules of the game. In the home education arena, these rules include the requirements specified in state law and local school district policy. The superintendents that we surveyed, however, did not appear to have a particularly clear or consistent understanding of home education laws. For instance, Table 6.1 shows that their reports of the school district's legal obligation to home educators varied substantially, even when the laws and policies among the states were relatively consistent.

Furthermore, superintendents' reports of their legal obligations to home-educating families varied substantially within each state. The Washington statute specifies several duties of local school district superintendents with respect to home education, including assessing parental qualifications, granting exemptions to operate home schools, and providing home-educated students access to ancillary services. Washington superintendents' responses about their obligations to home educators varied, however, from the narrow "only registration and ancillary services" to the broad "anything they need." In Washington and Utah, there were superintendents who reported that the public schools had no legal responsibilities regarding home education. Clearly much variation exists among superintendents' interpretation of their legal obligations to home-educating families, and consequently, the manner in which home schools are dealt with by various districts. We suggest that several factors were responsible for this variation: how superintendents learned about the home education law, their interactions with parent educators,

TABLE 6.1 Superintendents' Reports of Legal Obligations to
Home Educators (in percentages)

Obligations	Superintendents in Nevada, Washington, and Utah
Whatever they need	19
Cooperate with parents	25
Testing and curricular materials	62
Registration and ancillary services	21
Registration only	47
Ancillary services only	10
Only what law demands	10
Monitor parents	50
None	18
Other	9

NOTE: Totals do not equal 100. Respondents were asked to mark all categories that applied.

and their perceptions about parent educators and the quality of home schools.

How Superintendents Learned
About the Home Education Law

Reddin (1966) suggested that information obtained from a combination of written and verbal sources has the greatest potential for retention by school administrators. As Table 6.2 indicates, the majority of the superintendents in this study reported getting information in both ways, from policy documents and professional meetings. Yet, within and across states, they did not appear to have a clear and consistent understanding of home education law. This situation raises questions about where superintendents received their information about home education and about the scope and detail of the information they received.

When we asked superintendents where they first learned about home education law, most cited legal documents and routine

TABLE 6.2 Sources of Superintendents' Information About
Home Education (in percentages)

Sources	Washington	Utah	Nevada
Newspapers or magazines	83	70	86
Legal documents/legislation	83	90	71
Materials from home school			
support group	68	50	57
Research reports	62	50	42
Other	14	0	0

NOTE: Totals do not equal 100. Respondents were asked to mark all categories that applied.

professional sources, such as publications from state departments of education, professional meetings, or public hearings. Similarly, when asked where they routinely obtain information about home schools and the parents who operate them, they again mentioned state department of education policy and legal documents, as well as newspapers and magazines. Superintendents ranked research reports (including scholarly articles) as their least likely source of information.

These sources suggest several things about the quality of the information superintendents received. First, state departments of education generally distribute policy documents that are brief and to the point, covering only the essentials of an issue. Consequently, supporting details or background information that might help build a deeper or more complete understanding of home education are commonly edited out of documents before the superintendents ever receive them. Secondly, superintendents' knowledge of home education is likely to be influenced, at least in part, by the perspectives taken in the popular press. The media's often sensationalized and superficial treatment of home education, however, makes the usefulness of this source to superintendents somewhat questionable. It is not likely that media reports supply superintendents with the professional knowledge and expertise they need to effectively implement home education policy. Furthermore, superintendents are able to obtain these sources of information with very little proactive behavior. The information comes to them, usually in a format designed for easy reading, not for in-depth study or exploration.

Research reports and materials from home school support groups, on the other hand, offer some superintendents an additional source of information about home education. The research reports, however, are not widely disseminated and can be arcane in their use of academic jargon. In addition, obtaining them requires action on the part of school superintendents, which given the daily demands and constraints of their positions, is unlikely to occur. Home school support group materials are also difficult to obtain. The materials are rarely advertised or disseminated beyond the group membership. This may help explain why superintendents rely on research reports and support group materials for information about home schooling less often then they rely on media reports and legal documents.

Finally, we found no statistical relationship between how superintendents learn about the home education law in their states and their depth of understanding of it. Other factors, however, such as the statute's complexity, the length of time since its enactment, and the amount of direct implementation involvement by superintendents, are likely to affect superintendents' levels of understanding. It is plausible, then, that the degree of knowledge that superintendents have about the home school law governing their state is due to a combination of inadequate preparation through state channels and inadequate sources of information and materials.[2]

Superintendents' Views About Home Education

Social psychologists have long recognized the relationship between peoples' attitudes and their behaviors (e.g., Ajzen & Fishbein, 1977; Schuman & Johnson, 1976). Thus superintendents' perceptions of home-educating parents and home schools are likely to affect the manner in which superintendents implement home education policy, and examining how superintendents' attitudes regarding home schools are shaped becomes a significant point of inquiry.

The majority of superintendents in our study reported that they encourage contacts between themselves and home educators. Their interactions, however, are generally limited to the routine activity of granting exemptions to parent educators. In turn, the perceptions that many superintendents form about parents' motivations for home education are based on preconceived notions rather than on detailed discussions with the parent educators. For example, the survey asked superintendents why they thought parents chose to establish home schools. The majority cited "religion" and "dissatisfaction with public schools" as the dominant forces behind parents' decisions to educate children at home. Although some superintendents merely stated the reasons that they felt were motivating parents' home school decisions, many others had quite dogmatic responses:

> Parents teach their children at home to keep them away from secular humanism influence. They believe that schools and communities at large are evil places.

> [Home school] parents are abusers of the system; they do it for child care reasons and because they are angry with the school system.

Although the survey allotted space for the superintendents to express their views about why these issues might compel parents to avoid public schools, few offered any explanation for their views. Similarly, superintendents did not offer any explanation when explicitly asked why they thought these factors would induce some parents to choose home education whereas many other parents with presumably similar sentiments would continue to send their children to public schools.

The superintendents' perceptions about why parents choose to teach their children at home are to some extent accurate. Some parents do choose home schooling for religious reasons or because they are dissatisfied with public schools. As we demonstrated in Chapters 3 and 4, however, parent educators' motivations for home education are more complex and detailed than the opinions offered by the superintendents in our study. Although parent educators often include religion and dissatisfaction with public schools as reasons for home education, they also frequently mention issues such as the desire to develop stronger bonds with their children and the wish to have greater control over their children's academic, social, and moral environment. Rather than citing only ideological motivations or negative perceptions of public schools, parents' responses focused on a range of issues that commonly tied the decision to home educate to particular "ways of life."

Further evidence suggests that parents' reasons for home education are multifaceted and go beyond religious opposition to public schools or self-imposed exile from them. In Chapter 5, for instance, we showed that some home-educating parents are using, or desire to use, public school facilities and services in their home school program. Other parents do not want their home school activities to be restricted by public school officials, but they look favorably on the idea of using public school facilities and services if their use of them is not regulated.

Superintendents' responses to our survey questions demonstrated little understanding of the home school population's diverse rationales for home education or the parents' contrasting sentiments about associating themselves with public schools. Awareness of the home school population's complexity was rarely demonstrated by superintendents to the degree shown by one superintendent in Nevada:

> Some parents want a religious education not provided by public or parochial schools for their children. Others distrust governmental authority in what they see as a personal and family matter. Other parents see [home schooling] as a way to provide their children an appropriate level of educational challenge. Our school district tries to ensure responsible programs of home schooling and to minimize antagonisms toward the school system. We recognize these parents as teachers and allow access to materials and in-service opportunities to those who wish to make use of them.

Superintendents' Perceptions
About the Quality of Home Schools

The laws in Washington, Nevada, and Utah allow for home education on the basis of educational equivalence with public schools. The curriculum, instruction, and assessment provided in the home school is expected to be roughly commensurate with the offerings in public schools. We asked superintendents to compare the quality of home schools and public schools on a variety of "educational equivalence" criteria, including quality of instruction, academics, facilities, time on task, student/teacher ratio, and individualized learning. Table 6.3 shows that the majority of superintendents ranked public schools as far superior to home schools in nearly every category of educational equivalence.

These beliefs on the part of superintendents are inconsistent not only with the basic arrangements and structures of the two kinds of schools but also with a large amount of available research that report high cognitive and noncognitive outcomes among home-educated children (Kelley, 1991; McGraw, 1989; Montgomery, 1989; Ray, 1990b; Shyers, 1992; Smedley, 1992). In fact, a common response among superintendents regarding the equivalency issue was one that eliminated the possibility of successful home schools:

Very few, if any, seem to diligently develop academic skills.

Home educators don't want any influence [over their children] other than parents; in my mind, they want to ensure their children's ignorance.

Home schoolers are generally people that have real emotional problems themselves. They need to realize the serious harm they are doing to their children in the long run, educationally and socially.

Given these perceptions, it might seem that superintendents would refuse, or certainly restrict, exemptions for home education on the basis of educational equivalence; doing otherwise would be to admit less than optimal performance by public schools. Such actions, however, are not the case. Despite the belief of many superintendents that home schools are inferior to public schools in nearly every respect, they continue to grant parents exemptions to home educate their children.

These decisions occur because superintendents feel the law gives them few alternatives. For example, educational equivalence crite-

TABLE 6.3 Superintendents' Ratings of Characteristics in Public Schools and Home Schools (in percentages)

Characteristic	Very Low	Low	Average	High	Very High
Quality of Teachers					
public schools	0	1	6	49	44
home schools	34	41	19	2	4
Adequate Facilities					
public schools	2	4	22	40	32
home schools	33	35	25	7	0
Time on Task					
public schools	0	2	28	54	17
home schools	22	32	31	12	3
Desirability of Student/Teacher Ratio					
public schools	2	13	30	20	35
home schools	23	4	4	11	60
Student Socialization					
public schools	0	0	20	44	37
home schools	51	41	8	1	0
Self-Esteem					
public schools	0	3	25	57	15
home schools	15	17	41	22	5
Individual Learning Programs					
public schools	0	5	35	47	13
home schools	11	10	20	26	33
Academic Standards					
public schools	1	3	21	52	24
home schools	20	27	37	15	1

NOTE: Totals may not equal 100 due to rounding.

ria are delineated vaguely in the states' laws. The laws focus more on minimal input issues, such as curriculum guidelines and length of school day, rather than on more substantive issues, such as facilities, materials, instructional processes, or student outcomes. It could be that the parent educators who challenged denials of exemptions to home educate on the basis of educational equivalence in the past make superintendents more likely to grant exemptions merely to avoid the trouble and expense of a lawsuit, regardless of their professional judgment (Knowles, 1989, 1991; Knowles et al., 1992; Mawdsley & Permuth, 1983).

Implications for Home Education Policy

A number of political and legislative indicators demonstrate that the current trend in the nation is to permit home educators access to a variety of public school facilities and services. Thus it is likely that superintendents will become more involved in home school policy implementation. If this does indeed become the case, superintendents (as well as other public educators, including classroom teachers and principals) will need to possess more than just a superficial understanding of home educators and the home education movement in order to make thoughtful, informed, and viable decisions.

Because many school district superintendents in this study have a vague and cursory understanding of their state's home education law, state departments of education should carefully examine, and perhaps reconsider, the kind of information on home education disseminated to superintendents. Superintendents are mired in reading material and home educators represent a numerically small constituency in local school districts, but these factors perhaps should not be dominant criteria in deciding how to treat home education in policy documents.

Furthermore, superintendents' misinterpretation of parents' intentions and motivations for home education could cause them to ignore the parents who are willing to establish cooperative relations with public schools. The data reported in Chapter 5 illustrate that although some parent educators want nothing to do with public schools, others are willing to take advantage of public school resources and services if informed of their availability and if the autonomy of the home-based instructional program is left intact. In addition, the many parents who reported that little information is exchanged between professional educators and home education parents (see Chapter 5) indicates that superintendents often play a reactive role in policy implementation. One superintendent elaborated on the degree to which he knew about the resource needs of the home education families in his district:

> Interactions with home school parents are generally limited to answering requests for information and offering explanations of state and district guidelines for home study. Such interactions occur at the time of the initial application. We rarely interact with the parents after that time.

It may not be reasonable or feasible to expect superintendents to seek out home educators, especially those parents who have intense ideological differences with public schools. It does seem appropriate, however, that when superintendents are in contact with home-educating families more than basic compliance issues should be discussed, particularly in states where parents are provided access to public school services and facilities.

Another significant finding was that superintendents exhibit little knowledge of the information supplied by the increasingly powerful home education networking organizations (see Chapter 2 for a discussion of these organizations), and they seemingly do not fully understand the political and informational power that parent educators possess through their networking endeavors.[3] This level of understanding could have serious ramifications, because home-educating parents have had tremendous success in the legislative arena in the past decade. As a result of their collective lobbying efforts, legislation permitting home education was passed in 27 states during the 1980s (Burgess, 1986). Given the current political tenor emphasizing school choice issues and taxpayer revolt, parent educators who feel they are not being accommodated by local school officials could prove to be a substantial force toward requiring full consideration of home educators by the professional education community. They represent a potentially active constituency that superintendents would be ill advised to ignore or inadvertently misjudge.

Notes

1. Several factors may have affected both the response rate and the nature of the respondents. First, the questionnaire was quite lengthy and required approximately 30 minutes to complete. This is a relatively long period of time in a busy superintendent's day. Several respondents wrote on the survey that they felt it was too long, and a few returned the blank instrument with comments about it being too long and a waste of their time. Second, superintendents who wished to avoid the topic of home schooling, either because of negativity or indifference toward its practice, or because they didn't feel informed enough about the topic, might have eschewed participation. Third, superintendents who have had little or no experience with home educators might have chosen not to complete the survey, believing that they had no relevant information to contribute. These limiting factors suggest that there may have been an oversampling of superintendents with a strong interest in (and possibly strong positive or negative sentiments about) home schooling.

2. Interestingly, a few superintendents learned of the law from parents who were activists involved in the Washington home-schooling movement.

3. In the early years of the home education movement, Raymond Moore's institute played a significant role in building an active coalition of parent educators. More recently, the activities of the National Center for Home Education and the Home School Legal Defense Association have been extensive. Both organizations have regular and extensive contact with home-educating parents and educational policy makers throughout the United States.

7

The Future of Home Schooling

I feel a little more confident now about home schooling my son. To some people [the task of home education] sounds monumental, as it did to me at first. But now it's not as big of a deal. Last week, I listened to women who were so excited that it was the first day of school. And I just kind of went, "Oh, I'm excited too. I'm excited to have my son at home with me." So, it's a different type of excitement.

—32-year-old home school mother, Washington

Throughout this book, we sought to give parent educators a voice by examining, from their perspectives, the multifaceted phenomenon of home education. With detailed description, we developed a sense of their diverse backgrounds and heterogeneous orientations to home schooling. We also described the types of facilities, services, and support that some parents feel are important to the operation of their home school, as well as the reasons why other parents have no desire to seek any resources from either conventional schools or the government.

In addition, we looked at how the implementation of the regulations governing home schools is associated with school superintendents' knowledge about home school policy and their impressions of the parents who operate home schools. As a result, we gave our full

99

attention to parent educators as a diverse population living within certain social and legal constraints.

The insights generated by the journey into the world of parent educators, however, often limited our ability to see the interrelationships between social life, school life, and family life. In this chapter, we briefly explore some of these interrelationships. We begin by discussing the relationship of the home school movement to the larger social order. We then raise policy issues and questions that acknowledge the importance of these relationships. We believe that this is a necessary first step if well-informed home education policies are to be developed. In the last part of the chapter, we suggest areas for future research.

The Social Context

The growth of the home school movement over the last several decades has prompted changing definitions of home education. In the early years of the movement, home education was typically defined as an educational deviancy or an act of religious fanaticism. Those definitions are gradually being replaced by more complex understandings of why increasing numbers of parents are choosing to home school their children. Although educating children at home is no longer viewed as a historical, social, or educational aberration, it is still commonly thought of as an incidental event.

The increasing popularity of home education, however, is not solely driven by the idiosyncratic behavior of parents who are dissatisfied with the public school system. Rather, home schooling is a way of organizing the education of one's children that holds particular meaning for parent educators. The significance that parents attribute to their home school activities varies from one social context to another, one family to another, and over time within individual families. Furthermore, the revitalized interest in home education bears a relationship to larger social trends.

The increasing number of home schools nationwide is occurring in a specific historical period, one that many social theorists characterize as centralized, technology driven, highly rational and bureaucratic, and morally fragmented. A distinguishing feature of contemporary society is the state's increasing intervention in private spheres of life (Habermas, 1987; Hunter, 1991; see Offe, 1985). The social movements of the 1970s and beyond (including the home school movement) emerged partially in response to these conditions.

The central issue around which the prevalent social movements of the era rally is individuals' right to defend particular worldviews to which they are committed (see Epstein, 1990). These movements range from the grassroots, or direct action, movements of the left (see Flacks, 1988) to the new religious movements of the right (see Hammond, 1985; Liebman & Wuthnow, 1983). Although their ideological differences are significant, they share common ground in their struggle against institutional dominance in the realms of culture, politics, the economy, and family life.

The social movements of today also embody particular moral understandings about existing ways of life (see Lorentzen, 1980; see also Page & Clelland, 1978). For example, some movements exalt particular political positions that reflect their participants' personal beliefs (as in the environmentalist movement). Other movements distinguish themselves from dominant cultural forms through fashion, music, or language (as in the countercultural movements of the 1960s and beyond). Still others aspire to put particular religious values at the center of social life (as in the activist fundamentalist movement). Thus the preservation, protection, and enhancement of particular worldviews are the common goals of many contemporary social movements (Flacks, 1988).

In many ways, the home school movement has goals similar to other social movements. The family, an important site of private life, stands in contrast to public institutions, and it offers individuals a protective environment in which to maintain and propagate their particular values and beliefs. When state regulations intrude upon family life, opposition is likely to emerge. For instance, many home-educating parents maintain political, educational, and religious beliefs that are incompatible with the organizational features of state schools. Some parents resist the liberalism and secular humanism associated with public schools, whereas others resist homogenized learning environments and standardized curricula. Home education allows parents to avoid such educational settings and to put their particular family values at the center of their children's educational experiences.

The home school movement, perhaps to an extent greater than other movements of the era, exemplifies the principles of individualism and self-reliance, and the attempt to live in a way that is consistent with one's worldview. The parents' perspectives that make up this book suggest that the movement is built on the belief that parents have a right to decide how their children will be educated and a right to control the types of socialization experiences and curricula to which their children will be exposed. In this sense, the home school movement acts in response to the "colonization" of the family by institutional forms such as public education. It protects family values and beliefs from state intrusion while simultaneously expanding the personal rights of parents by permitting them to adopt freely chosen lifestyles. (See Habermas, 1987, for an informative discussion on the institutional "colonization of the life world" and its effect on modern society.)

The individualism that is a core feature of the home school movement, however, does not negate home-educating parents' strong sense of family and community. They are strongly committed to the education of their children, the extended home education community, and in some cases, particular religious communities. In turn, home-educating parents develop close bonds with family and community members. The question, therefore, is not whether home-educating parents will withdraw from the public sphere, but to what extent and in what manner will they remain involved in the public sphere? Debates around this issue undoubtedly will continue as home school policies are being established.

Policy Considerations

The struggle over home school policy is rooted in the competing moral visions of parent educators and the professional educational establishment. Although the struggles seem of staggering magnitude, the possibility that moral differences can be accommodated by opening a public discourse is a useful idea. Indeed, as James Hunter (1991) argued in his book *Culture Wars*, "without a common belief that public standards do exist and without a commitment to determine what they are, there is no basis for making public compromises" (p. 29).

The explicit purpose of the questions we raise below is to develop such a discourse. The point of our ruminations is to challenge educational policy makers, parent educators, and professional educators, as well as all who are interested in the education of children, to rethink the relationship between personal interests and public practices. In asking these questions, we are not suggesting that home school students be assimilated into conventional schools or totally abandoned by them. We do not regard the regulations that require home-educating parents to be accountable to public schools as the best or only strategy that can be developed to serve the common good. In light of the parents' perspectives presented throughout this book, these approaches are unwarranted and probably ineffectual. We believe that if parent and professional educators fail to articulate their moral obligations, then misunderstanding and intolerance will prevail. The challenge is to understand more fully what divides these groups and to develop well-informed policies that foster cooperation and preclude further polarization. We begin to meet this challenge by raising issues and questions regarding the relationship between home schools and conventional schools.

Opening a Dialogue: Issues and Questions

Issue 1: Home education parents want to be intimately involved in the education of their children. Professional educators also desire parental involvement in the educational affairs of children, and they spend much effort establishing programs to reach that goal.

✓ What are the many nuances to the concept of parental involvement? To what extent do professional educators conceive of parental involvement as being more than homework supervision? How do they perceive the presence of parents assisting in the classroom (e.g., do they regard it as helpful, a nuisance, invasion of their privacy)?

✓ To what extent could parent educators assist parents who are attempting to become more involved in their children's conventional school education, even though they wish to continue educating their own children at home?

✓ To what extent do professional educators accept and act upon the possibility that many home-educating parents have close knowledge of their children's educational needs, despite the fact that most are not professionally certified educators? Conversely, to what extent do home-educating parents accept and act upon the possibility that many professional educators have sound insights about educational matters?

✓ How could children benefit from the educational insights of both professional educators and home-educating parents?

Issue 2: Home school parents are highly focused on the educational progress of their children. They make extensive time, energy, and financial commitments to their children's educational welfare. Yet, most seem reluctant to become involved with other educational communities.

✓ How can public and private schools capitalize on the enthusiasm and commitment home school parents exhibit in the education of their children?

✓ To what extent could parent educators be included, as members of communities, in conventional school decision-making processes? To what extent, if any, should home school parents be involved in the formation of local educational policy and implementation?

✓ Are there ways to involve successful parent educators in formal school settings as instructional leaders or as resources for the professional development activities offered to professional educators?

Issue 3: We acknowledge that the core of home school parents are adamant that their children will never attend conventional schools. In addition, we recognize that there is a sizable group who made the decision to home educate their children because of the particular conditions that they and/or their children experienced in conventional schools. In the future, some of these parents may wish to reconsider the appropriateness of public (or private) schools for their children.

✓ In what ways could information about home educational activities be useful to teachers in public (or private) schools who help children make the transition from home school to conventional school?

✓ What kinds of procedures could conventional schools implement to facilitate dialogues with parents who home school for only short periods of time and to assist these parent educators in making well-informed educational decisions for their children?

✓ In what ways could parent educators establish ongoing contacts with professional educators that may be beneficial if their children later enroll in conventional schools?

Issue 4: Many home-educating parents are strongly committed to home instruction and are not inclined to enroll their children in public schools. Some of these parents, however, recognize that school districts and other community agencies have resources from which they and their children could benefit. Often though, parent educators are unaware of the resources that are available to them and their children and do not know to what degree the resources would be accessible for their use at their own discretion.

✓ How can professional educators and community resource agencies make known their willingness to assist the home school community?

✓ How can professional educators, community resource agencies, and home-educating parents work together to develop the plan of resource utilization that will benefit children the most?

✓ How can home-educating parents better inform professional educators and community resource agencies about the services that they would like to have available for home schools and the extent to which they would like to utilize those services in a nonregulated fashion?

Issue 5: Home school parents are well educated as a group and have many ideas about teaching and learning. Similarly, professional educators are well educated as a group and have many ideas about teaching and learning.

✓ What are the differences between teaching, guiding, and facilitating children's learning at home versus in a conventional classroom? How can those differences be recognized and put to beneficial use by all who are concerned with children's educational welfare?

✓ In what ways can professional educators learn from home educators and not feel threatened by parents' perceptions of how children best learn?

✓ In what ways can home-educating parents learn from professional educators without rejecting professionals' knowledge of childhood learning?

✓ How can professional educators' knowledge about classroom learning environments and home educators' knowledge about home
learning environments be used to inform each other's thinking?

✓ What kind of forum could bring the most effective home-educating
parents and the most effective public school teachers together for
the purposes of rethinking the relationship between public education and home-based education?

Issue 6: Home-educating parents place a high degree of importance on the social and moral environment within which learning
takes place. Professional educators, however, often argue that the
home is an extremely restrictive learning environment that may
damage the social development of children.

✓ How do home school and conventional school parents' concepts of
what constitutes appropriate social and moral climates differ from
each other? How are their concepts similar to each other?

✓ How can parents and professional educators assist each other in
fostering social and moral environments in conventional schools
that are acceptable to both parties?

✓ How could the involvement of home education parents and their
children in conventional school programs help develop a social
environment for home-educated children that is acceptable to both
parties?

Issue 7: Home school communities are largely composed of white,
Anglo, middle-class families. Other racial, ethnic, and income groups
are involved, however. These groups, nevertheless, may not have
access to broad levels of social support, and they may feel alienated
by the predominantly white, middle-class, Anglo leadership in national, regional, and local networking organizations.

✓ What might be done by local, statewide, and national home education leaders to facilitate the development of a hospitable and successful home-schooling environment for minority and low-income
families?

✓ How can professional educators better assist minority and low-income
families in their endeavors to educate their children at home?

✓ To what extent do minority parents who home educate replicate
white, Anglo parent educators' thinking about public schools? In
what ways is the thinking of these groups different?

✓ What can professional educators learn from minority parents who remove their children from conventional schools in order to educate them at home?

✓ Given the limited resources of many low-income families, are school districts more or less sensitive to the intents of lower-income home-educating parents than they are to the intents of middle-class home-educating parents?

Learning More:
Research Suggestions

Our questions only begin to demonstrate the vast research opportunities that are available to educational and social science researchers. During our years of exploring home education, we found that for each question we pursued, several new questions emerged. For instance, in this chapter, we chose to focus on issues and questions that maximize the possibility of opening a dialogue between home-educating parents and professional educators. More research is needed, however, to determine how these questions will be negotiated and answered. To what extent are the principles of each alliance nonnegotiable? To what degree will differences in values and moral obligations be accepted and acted upon? It is conceivable that the researchers who pursue these questions and formulate answers to them will play an instrumental role in the types of negotiations that occur between home-educating parents and professional educators.

Other research remains to be done on parent educators. Although this study explored the lifestyle concerns of home-educating parents, what made these *particular* parents activate the home school option is still unclear. We know of Christian Evangelical parents who oppose the secular nature of public schools, yet decide to voice their concerns in public debates and protests rather than removing their children from conventional schools (see Page & Clelland, 1978; Provenzo, 1990). We also know of many parents who continue to send their children to public schools even though they have concerns similar to those of home-educating parents about the moral climate of public schools and the socialization experiences that their children may encounter in public schools (Brandt, 1993; *Phi Delta Kappan*, 1990). Furthermore, we know of many families who send their children to public schools although they do not support the educational and social policies rendered by federal, state, and local governments. We also know of families who have little confidence in mainstream social institutions, yet they continue to enroll their children in conventional schools (NORC, 1990). Future research needs to examine why particular families activate the option of home schooling, but others with similar concerns, moral understandings, and ways of life do not. A model developed by Mayberry (1991) proposes various micro and macro structural elements that could be used to begin addressing this question.

More research is also needed to examine what goes on inside home schools. There is some evidence to suggest that during the initial phases of home schooling, parents tend to replicate traditional classroom teaching styles. It appears, however, that the traditional model is soon replaced with a much more flexible and child-centered model (Taylor, 1993; Van Galen, 1988). There is little research to explain why this transition occurs or examine the various styles and methods parents use to educate their children at home. Research in this area would advance our understanding of the educational processes that are associated with home schools and the potential strengths and weaknesses of differing home-based instructional programs.

Research that examines the procedures typically used to evaluate the effectiveness of home-based educational programs is also warranted. The appropriateness of using state-mandated methods of assessing home-educated children's achievement is questionable (see Cizek, 1991, 1993). Studies need to be conducted that explore the ability of alternative assessment methods, such as performance assessments (i.e., assessments based on student projects, portfolios, speeches, essays, oral reports, etc.), to evaluate the overall quality of home education programs.

Research is also needed to determine the trials and tribulations of cooperative programs such as those mentioned in Chapter 5. These studies could inform school officials and home school parents about the potential benefits and drawbacks of cooperative programs and provide models for the development of future programs. As more cooperation between local school districts (or private schools) and home schools occurs, it will be increasingly important to conduct evaluation studies of these programs. Researchers, however, must be sensitive to the diversity of reasons parents have for home schooling and they must acknowledge that many parents will not want to engage in cooperative activities.

Finally, children are the most overlooked group in the home education literature. The possibilities are endless for research that takes into account children's perceptions about receiving their schooling at home.

An Image for the Future

When we started researching home schools, we were preoccupied with the question: Why do parents teach their children at home? The diversity of answers that we received, coupled with the enduring nature of home education, inspired us to think more broadly about home education. We became more concerned about identifying the ways in which the home education movement could teach us something about the relationship between family life, school life, and social life in an increasingly complex and diverse society. Consequently, our interests became driven by a new set of questions: What is the relationship between home education and family values and worldviews? What role do particular values and views play in the home education community, conventional schools, and the larger social order? What evokes the tenuous relationship between home-educating parents and professional educators? What new ways of thinking about education can we imagine that acknowledges individual liberty and preserves the notion of public obligation? (See Lines, 1993, for a preliminary commentary on this issue.)

When we think about these questions and reflect upon our associations with home school families over the years, we are again reminded of the many parent educators who explained to us the complex reasons they had for teaching their children at home. We are also reminded of the emotionally charged meetings attended by home-educating parents and the educational officials who developed state and local home school policies. The meetings were often antagonistic and generally counterproductive. They did not serve the common goal of parent educators and professional educators: to protect a child's right to the best possible education.

These experiences heightened our interest in finding ways to open a dialogue between the two groups, a dialogue that acknowledged diverse ways of educating children. The recognition of parent educators' perspectives about teaching their children at home is the first step toward that goal. It is our sincere hope that the issues and questions we raised in this chapter and throughout the book inspire among all those interested in the education of children a "language of possibility" (Freire, 1970). The hope for the advancement of any marginalized group lies in developing a sense of what is possible.

References

Ajzen, I., & Fishbein, M. (1977). Attitude-behavior relations: A theoretical analysis and review of empirical research. *Psychological Bulletin, 84*, 888-918.

Allis, S. (1990, October 22). Schooling kids at home. *Time*, pp. 84, 86.

Arnold, D. O. (1970). Dimensional sampling: An approach for studying a small number of cases. *American Sociologist, 5*, 147-150.

Astin, A. W. (1992). Educational "choice": Its appeal may be illusory. *Sociology of Education, 65*, 255-259.

Avner, J. A. (1989). Home schoolers: A forgotten clientele? *School Library Journal, 35*, 29-33.

Baker, J. S., Jr. (1988). Parent-centered education. *Notre Dame Journal of Law, Ethics, and Public Policy, 3*, 535-568.

Bastian, A., Fruchter, N., Gittel, M., Greer, C., & Haskins, K. (1985). *Choosing equality: The case for democratic schooling.* Philadelphia: Temple University Press.

Bates, V. (1991). Lobbying for the Lord: The new Christian right home-schooling movement and grassroots lobbying. *Review of Religious Research, 33*, 3-17.

Beckford, J. A. (1984). Holistic imagery and ethics in religious and healing movements. *Social Compass, 31*, 259-272.

Bishop, C. (1991). Home schooling parent support groups in Kansas: A naturalistic inquiry into their concerns and functions. *Home School Researcher, 7*, 11-16.

Brandt, R. S. (Ed.). (1993). Contemporary issues: Public schools and the Christian fundamentalists [Special issue]. *Educational Leadership, 51*, 4, 5, 6-11, 12-15, 16-21, 22-23, 24-28, 30-34, 35, 36, 38-40, 41-43.

Bumstead, R. A. (1979). Educating your child at home: The Perchemlides case. *Phi Delta Kappan, 2*, 97-100.

Burgess, K. T. (1986). The constitutionality of home education statutes. *UMKC Law Review, 55,* 69-84.

Burrow v. State, 669 S.W.2d 441 (Ark. 1984).

Campbell, R., Cunningham, L., Nystrand, R., & Usdan, M. (1985). *The organization and control of American schools.* Columbus, OH: Charles E. Merrill.

Care and Protection of Charles, 399 Mass. 324 (1987).

Carper, J. (1983). The Christian day school movement. *Educational Forum, 47,* 135-148.

Churbuck, D. C. (1993, October 11). The ultimate school choice: No school at all. *Forbes,* pp. 144, 145, 148-150.

Cizek, G. J. (1991). Alternative assessments: Promises and problems for home-based education policy. *Home School Researcher, 7,* 13-21.

Cizek, G. J. (1993). The mismeasure of home schooling effectiveness: A commentary. *Home School Researcher, 9,* 1-4.

Coleman, J. S. (1988). Social capital in the creation of human capital. *American Journal of Sociology, 94,* S95-S120.

Coleman, J. S. (1992). Some points on choice in education. *Sociology of Education, 65,* 260-262.

Coleman, J. S., & Hoffer, T. (1987). *Public and private high schools: The impact of communities.* New York: Basic Books.

Colfax, D. J., & Colfax, M. (1988). *Homeschooling for excellence.* New York: Warner.

Collin, M. (1983, December 12). District has uneasy alliance with home schools. *Salt Lake Tribune,* p. A14.

Cooper, B., McLaughlin, D., & Manno, B. (1983). The latest word on private-school growth. *Teachers College Record, 85,* 88-98.

Cremin, L. A. (1977). *Traditions of American education.* New York: Basic Books.

Dalaimo, D. (in press). Community home education: A case-study of a public school-based home schooling program. *Educational Research Quarterly.*

Delahooke, M. (1986). Home educated children's social/emotional adjustment and academic achievement: A comparative study. *Dissertation Abstracts International, 47,* 475A.

DeJonges celebrated victory at Michigan supreme court. (1993, May/June). *Home School Court Report, 9,* 1, 2.

Delconte v. State, 329 S.E.2d 636 (N.C. 1985).

Divoky, D. (1983). The pioneers of the home-schooling movement. *Phi Delta Kappan, 64,* 395-398.

Dougherty, K., & Hammack, F. (1990). *Education and society.* New York: Harcourt Brace Jovanovich.

Education Commission of the States. (1983). *Action for excellence: A comprehensive plan to improve our nation's schools* (ERIC ED 235 588). Denver, CO: Author.

Employment Division, Department of Human Resources of Oregon et al. v. Smith et al., 494 U.S. 872, 108 L.Ed.2d 876, 110 S.Ct. 1595, reh. den., (U.S.) 110 L.Ed.2d 285, 110 S.Ct. 2605 (1990).

Epstein, B. (1990). Rethinking social movement theory. *Socialist Review, 20,* 35-65.

Farrington v. Tokushige, 273 U.S. 284 (1927).

Flacks, R. (1988). *Making history.* New York: Columbia University Press.

Fleisher, D., & Freedman, D. M. (1983). *Death of an American: The killing of John Singer.* New York: Continuum.

Freire, P. (1970). *The pedagogy of the oppressed* (M. B. Ramos, Trans.). New York: Herder & Herder.

Gladin, W. E. (1987). *Home education: Characteristics of its families and schools*. Unpublished doctoral dissertation, Bob Jones University, Greensborough, SC.

Gordon, E., & Gordon, E. (1990). *Centuries of tutoring: A history of alternative education in America and Western Europe*. Lanham, MD: University Press of America.

Growing Without Schooling. (1994, January/February). P. 37.

Gustavsen, G. A. (1981). Selected characteristics of home schools and parents who operate them. *Dissertation Abstracts International, 42*, 4381-4382A.

Guterson, D. (1990, November). When schools fail children. *Harper's Magazine*, 58-64.

Habermas, J. (1987). *The theory of communicative action* (Vol. 2). Boston: Beacon Press.

Hadeed, H. (1991). Home schooling movement participation: A theoretical framework. *Home School Researcher, 7*, 1-9.

Hammond, P. E. (Ed.). (1985). *The sacred in a secular age*. Berkeley: University of California Press.

Hannigan, J. A. (1988, October). *Ideological affinity and social movement networks: The case of "New Age" spirituality*. Paper presented at the annual meeting of the Association for the Sociology of Religion, Atlanta, GA.

Hargrove, B. (1988). Religion, development, and changing paradigms. *Sociological Analysis, 49*, S33-S48.

Harris, J., & Fields, R. (1982). Outlaw generation: A legal analysis of the home-instruction movement. *Educational Horizons, 61*, 26-51.

Havens, J. E. (1991). *A study of parent education levels as they relate to academic achievement among home schooled children*. Unpublished doctoral (Ed.D.) dissertation, Southwestern Baptist Theological Seminary, Fort Worth, TX.

Hedin, N. S. (1991). Self-concept of Baptist children in three educational settings. *Home School Researcher, 7*, 1-5.

Holt, J. (1969). *The underachieving school*. New York: Dell.

Holt, J. (1983). Schools and home schoolers: A fruitful partnership. *Phi Delta Kappan, 64*, 391-394.

Holt, J. (1984, January/February). So you want to home-school. *Mother Earth News*, 139-141.

Home School Court Report. (1993, November/December). P. 11.

Home schooling: The best education. (1992, September 28). *Los Angeles Times*, p. B4.

Hunter, J. D. (1991). *Culture wars: The struggle to define America*. New York: Basic Books.

Illich, I. (1970). *Deschooling society*. New York: Harper Colophon.

Kachel, D. (1989). How the Amish educate their children: Can we learn from them? *Educational Horizons, 67*, 92-97.

Kaseman, S., & Kaseman, L. (1990). *Taking charge through home schooling: Personal and political empowerment*. Stoughton, WI: Koshkonong.

Kaseman, S., & Kaseman, L. (1991, January/February). Does home schooling research help home schooling? *Home Education Magazine*, 26-27, 46-49.

Kelley, S. W. (1991). Socialization of home schooled children: A self-concept study. *Home School Researcher, 7*, 1-12.

King, G. M. (1983). Home schooling: Up from underground. *Reason, 14*(12), 21-29.

Klicka, C. (1990, August). *Home schooling in the United States: A statutory analysis*. Paeonian Springs, VA: Home School Legal Defense Association.

Knight, M. (1987). Parental liberties versus the state's interest in education: The case for allowing home education. *Texas Tech Law Review, 18*, 1261-1289.

Knowles, J. G. (1989). Cooperating with home school parents: A new agenda for public schools? *Urban Education, 23,* 392-411.

Knowles, J. G. (1991). Parents' rationales for operating home schools. *Journal of Contemporary Ethnography, 20,* 203-230.

Knowles, J. G., Marlow, S. E., & Muchmore, J. A. (1992). From pedagogy to ideology: Origins and phases of home schools in the United States, 1970-1990. *American Journal of Education, 100,* 195-235.

Knowles, J. G., Mayberry, M., & Ray, B. (1991). *An assessment of home schools in Nevada, Oregon, Utah, and Washington: Implications for public education and a vehicle for informed policy decision, summary report* (U.S. Department of Education Field Initiated Research Project Grant No. R117E90220).

Kohn, A. (1988, April). Home schooling: Parents who educate their children at home face little official opposition—but a very demanding responsibility. *Atlantic,* pp. 20-25.

Liebman, R., & Wuthnow, R. (Eds.). (1983). *The new Christian right.* New York: Aldine.

Lines, P. A. (1982). State regulation of private education. *Phi Delta Kappan, 64,* 119-123.

Lines, P. A. (1983). Private education and state regulation. *Journal of Law and Education, 12,* 189-234.

Lines, P. A. (1985a). *Compulsory education laws and their impact on public and private education.* Denver, CO: Education Commission of the States.

Lines, P. A. (1985b, May 15). States should help, not hinder, parents' home-schooling efforts. *Education Week,* pp. 17, 24.

Lines, P. A. (1986, January 15). Home school researcher affirms validity of data. *Education Week,* p. 26.

Lines, P. A. (1991a). *Estimating the home schooled population* (Working paper OR 91-537). Washington DC: Office of Educational Research and Improvement, U.S. Department of Education.

Lines, P. A. (1991b). Home instruction: The size and growth of the movement. In J. A. Van Galen & M. A. Pitman (Eds.), *Home schooling: Political, historical, and pedagogical perspectives* (pp. 9-41). Norwood, NJ: Ablex.

Lines, P. A. (1993). *Homeschooling: Private choices and public obligations* (Working paper). Washington DC: Office of Educational Research and Improvement, U.S. Department of Education.

Lorentzen, L. (1980). Evangelical life style concerns expressed in political action. *Sociological Analysis, 21,* 32-41.

Lupu, I. C. (1987). Home education, religious liberty, and the separation of powers. *Boston University Law Review, 6,* 971-990.

Marlow, S. E. (1992). *Home schools, public schools, politics, and practice: Superintendents' implementation of home education policy in four Western states.* Unpublished doctoral dissertation, University of Michigan, Ann Arbor.

Mawdsley, R., & Permuth, S. (1983). State regulation of religious schools: A need for direction. *NOLPE School Law Journal, 11,* 55-63.

Mayberry, M. (1988). Doing it their way: A study of Oregon's home schoolers. *Dissertation Abstracts International, 44*(12), 3457A.

Mayberry, M. (1989). Home-based education in the United States: Demographics, motivations and educational implications. *Educational Review, 41,* 171-180.

Mayberry, M. (1991, April). *Deschooling society: A study of home schools in 4 western states.* Paper presented at the Department of Sociology Spring Colloquium, University of Oregon.

Mayberry, M. (1992). Home-based education: Parents as teachers. *Continuing Higher Education Review, 56,* 48-58.

Mayberry, M. (1993). Effective learning environments in action: The case of home schools. *School Community Journal, 3,* 61-68.

Mayberry, M., & Gerdes, E. (1989). Home schooling in Nevada: Current state law, implementation, and proposed refinements. *Inter Alia: Journal of the State Bar of Nevada, 54,* 16-20.

Mayberry, M., & Knowles, J. G. (1989). Family unity of parents who teach their children: Ideological and pedagogical orientations to home schooling. *Urban Review, 21,* 209-226.

McGraw, R. K. (1989). Selected aspects of home-schooling as reported by home-schooling parents and reported with perceptions of Indiana public school superintendents and principals of home-schooling in Indiana. *Dissertation Abstracts International, 50,* 2736A.

Merrill, D. (1983, September). Schooling at mother's knee: Can it compete? *Christianity Today, 2,* 16-21.

Meyer v. Nebraska, 262 U.S. 390 (1923).

Montgomery, L. (1989). The effect of homeschooling on the leadership skills of home-schooled students. *Home School Researcher, 5,* 1-10.

Moore, R. S. (1983). Letter to John Holt: How many are we? *Growing Without Schooling, 32,* 14-16.

Naisbitt, J. (1982). *Megatrends.* New York: Warner.

National Commission on Excellence in Education. (1983). *A nation at risk* (ERIC ED 226 006). Washington, DC: Government Printing Office.

National Opinion Research Center. (1990). *General social surveys, 1972-1990: Cumulative codebook.* Chicago: University of Chicago.

Natriello, G., McDill, E., & Pallas, A. (1985). School reform and potential dropouts. *Educational Leadership, 2,* 161-166.

Offe, C. (1985). New social movements: Challenging the boundaries of institutional politics. *Social Research, 52,* 817-868.

Page, A., & Clelland, D. (1978). The Kanawha County textbook controversy: A study of the politics of life style concern. *Social Forces, 57,* 265-281.

Pastor jailed for home educating. (1987, February 22). *Salt Lake Tribune,* p. A5.

People v. DeJonge, 501 N.W.2d 127 (Mich. 1993).

Perchemlides v. Frizzle, No. 16641 (Mass. Hampshire County Superior Court, 1978).

Phi Delta Kappan. (1990). The 20th annual gallup poll, *70,* 33-38.

Pierce v. Society of Sisters, 268 U.S. 510 (1925).

Pitman, M. A. (1987). Compulsory education and home schooling: Truancy or prophesy? *Education and Urban Society, 19,* 280-289.

Postman, N., & Weingartner, C. (1973) *How to recognize a good school.* Bloomington, IN: Phi Delta Kappa.

Provenzo, E. F. (1990). *Religious fundamentalism and American education.* New York: State University of New York Press.

Quine, D., & Marek, E. (1988). Reasoning abilities of home-educated children. *Home School Researcher, 4,* 1-6.

Ray, B. (1988). Home schools: A synthesis of research on characteristics and learner outcomes. *Education and Urban Society, 21,* 16-31.

Ray, B. D. (1990a). *Home education in Montana: Family characteristics and student achievement.* Salem, OR: National Home Education Research Institute.

Ray, B. D. (1990b). *A nationwide study of home education: Family characteristics, legal matters, and student achievement.* Salem, OR: National Home Education Research Institute.

Ray, B. D. (1990c, April). *An overview of home schooling in the United States: Its growth and development and future challenges.* Paper presented at the annual meeting of the American Educational Research Association, San Francisco.

Ray B. D. (1992a). *Marching to the beat of their own drum: A profile of home education research.* Salem, OR: National Home Education Research Institute.

Ray, B. D. (1992b, April). *On the propriety of education professionals instructing home educators.* Paper presented at the annual meeting of the American Educational Research Association, San Francisco.

Ray, B. D., & Wartes, J. (1991). The academic achievement and affective development of home-schooled children. In J. A. Van Galen & M. A. Pitman (Eds.), *Home schooling: Political, historical and pedagogical perspectives* (pp. 43-62). Norwood, NJ: Ablex.

Reddin, W. J. (1966). The tri-dimensional grid. *Canadian Personnel and Industrial Relations Journal, 13,* 13-20.

Richardson, S., & Zirkel, P. (1991). Home schooling law. In J. A. Van Galen & M. A. Pitman (Eds.), *Home schooling: Political, historical and pedagogical perspectives* (pp. 159-210). Norwood, NJ: Ablex.

Ritter, M. (1979, October). Read this before you veto home-education requests. *American School Board Journal,* 38-40.

Roach, V. (1989, February). Home schooling in times of educational reform. *Education Digest,* pp. 58-61.

Rowe, J. (1987, April). Alternative education. *Christian Science Monitor, 24,* 6-10.

San Diego County Office of Education. (1988). *Home education parent handbook.* San Diego, CA: Author.

San Diego County Office of Education. (1990). *School accountability report card.* San Diego, CA: Author.

Schuman, H., & Johnson, M. P. (1976). Attitudes and behavior. *Annual Review of Sociology, 2,* 161-207.

Scoma v. Chicago Board of Education, 391 F.Supp. 452 (N.D. Ill. 1974).

Seligmann, J., & Abramson, P. (1988, February). From homespun to Harvard: The California Colfaxes teach their children well. *Newsweek,* p. 49.

Sexson, B. (1988). *Home schooling: A socio-educational analysis of an emergent cultural shift in consciousness.* Ann Arbor, MI: University Microfilms.

Shepherd, M. (1986). The home schooling movement: An emerging conflict in American education [abstract]. *Home School Researcher, 2,* 1.

Shupe, A., & Stacey, W. (1983). The moral majority constituency. In R. Liebman & R. Wuthnow (Eds.), *The new Christian right* (pp. 103-115). New York: Aldine.

Shyers, L. E. (1992). A comparison of social adjustment between home and traditionally schooled students. *Home School Researcher, 8,* 1-8.

Smedley, T. (1992). Socialization of home school children. *Home School Researcher, 8,* 9-16.

Smith, B. (1990). *American science policy since World War II.* Washington, DC: Brookings Institution.

Smith, M., & Klicka, C. (1987). Review of Ohio law regarding home school. *Ohio Northern University Law Review, 87,* 301-328.

Stevens, C. W. (1979, September 13). Angry at schools, more parents try teaching at home. *Wall Street Journal,* pp. 1, 33.

Stocklin-Enright, B. (1982). The constitution of home education: The role of the parent, the state and the child. *Willamette Law Review, 18,* 558-611.

Taylor, J. W. (1987). Self-concept in home-schooling children. *Dissertation Abstracts International, 47,* 2809A.

Taylor, L. A. (1993). *At home in school: A qualitative inquiry into three Christian home schools.* Unpublished doctoral dissertation, Stanford University, Stanford, CA.

Tobak, J. W., & Zirkel, P. A. (1982). Home instruction: An analysis of the statutes and case law. *University of Dayton Law Review, 8,* 1-59.

Toch, T., Wagner, B., Johnson, C., Glastris, K., Arrarte, A., & Daniel, M. (1991, December 9). The exodus [from public schools]. *U.S. News & World Report, 111*(24), 66-77.

Treat, E. (1990). Parents teaching reading and writing at home: An ethnographic study. *Home School Researcher, 6,* 9-19.

Twentieth Century Fund Task Force on Federal Elementary and Secondary Education Policy. (1983). *Making the grade* (ERIC ED 233 112). New York: Author.

U.S. Bureau of the Census. (1990). *1990 census of population social and economic characteristics* (Documents No. CP-2-30, CP-2-46, CP-2-49). Washington, DC: Author.

U.S. Bureau of the Census. (1993). *Statistical abstracts of the United States* (113th ed.). Washington DC: Author.

Van Galen, J. A. (1986). *Schooling in private: A study of home education.* Unpublished doctoral dissertation, University of North Carolina, Chapel Hill.

Van Galen, J. A. (1988). Becoming home schoolers. *Urban Education, 23,* 89-106.

Vergon, C. B. (1986). *The church, the state, and the schools: Contemporary issues in law and policy.* Ann Arbor: University of Michigan School of Education.

Victories for home schooling. (1989, April 9). *New York Times,* p. 26.

Wartes, J. (1988) *Report from the 1987 Washington home school testing.* Woodinville, WA: Washington Homeschool Research Project.

Wartes, J. (1990a). *The relationship of selected input variables to academic achievement among Washington's homeschoolers.* Woodinville, WA: Washington Homeschool Research Project.

Wartes, J. (1990b). *Report from the 1986 through 1989 Washington homeschool testing.* Woodinville, WA: Washington Homeschool Research Project.

Williamson, D. (1979). *School at home: An alternative to public schooling.* Bend, OR: Maverick.

Wisconsin v. Yoder, 406 U.S. 205 (1972).

Yastrow, S. (1990). Home instruction: A national study of state law. *Home School Researcher, 6,* 13-18.

Index